Cheap CHIC

by
Caterine Milinaire
and Carol Troy

Designed by Bea Feitler

Harmony Books
New York

Publisher: Bruce Harris
Editor: Linda Sunshine
Production: Gene Conner, Murray Schwartz
Book and Cover Design: Bea Feitler
Design Assistant: Carl Barile
Research: Martha Siegler, Diane Partie
Cover Lettering: Barbara Richer
Cover Photograph of Jerry Hall by Bill King

Harmony Books, a division of Crown Publishers, Inc.
419 Park Avenue South, New York, N.Y. 10016

Published simultaneously in Canada by General Publishing Company Limited.
Printed in the United States of America.

Library of Congress Cataloging in Publication Data

Milinaire, Caterine.
Cheap chic.

1. Fashion.   2. Clothing and dress.
I. Troy, Carol, joint author.   II. Title
TT515.M59   646'.34   75-25562
ISBN 0-517-52453-8
ISBN 0-517-52368-X pbk.

TABLE OF CONTENTS

dedicated to

maurice · hogenboom

from caterine

6

First, thanks to my parents, who kept me in cowboy clothes as a kid (and had my teeth straightened besides); thanks to Tom Werts, the first man I knew to wear fatigues; to Helene Gaillet and her new Leica; to the Ali-Bonavena fight for bringing me to *Rags* magazine and Jon Carroll, John Burks, Mary Peacock, Blair Sabol and Hope Mell; to Velveteen Rose and Frank Robertson for many companionable evenings; to Clive Irving and Pucci Meyer at *Newsday*; to you people in Chicago who know who you are, especially Melinda and John; to the World's Largest Souvenir Shop in Galveston, Texas, where I got my first running jump on this book; to Louise at Stelzig's and Brett and country music; to my pastel pink 1963 Mercury Monterey with the electric back window and 6 AM trips to the Sausalito Flea Market; to the fifth floor of

the Chateau Marmont, shag rug and all; to Lexington Labs; to everybody on Western Avenue and Lala too; to Kawasaki, my favorite bike; to Cathy Breslin, whose good friendship kept me plugging and slugging; to people who tell you that nothing beats a miss like a try; to Andrea and Alain Adam in London; to Francois for lending his closet and John Lombardi and Tina Bossidy for lending their sense of style; to the Polio Lounge and Steve from Warner Brothers; to the fast yellow Caddy and fishing at Marathon Key; to dinners at Mi Tierra, mussels at Elaine's and drinks at Nicola's (where we couldn't get a table); to Inglenook chablis, good, like most things from California; to Rosalee Wright and the sporting life; to Diane Partie and Martha Siegler for fast fingers and tough minds; to Caterine, Buzios Bea and all the people at Harmony; to Uncle Hugh Troy for having written such lovely little books; to Raymond Chandler for his heightened sense of romance; to Jack Nessel for living in Paris; to the psychic in the South who told me this book would make us all a lot of money and also be a Force for Good; and to those damned devils. Thanks for the memories.
Carol Troy/August 1975.

INTRODUCTION

Personal style is what this book is all about. Fashion as a dictatorship of the elite is dead. Nobody knows better than you what you should wear or how you should look. What we want to do is to lay out the alternatives, the guidelines, and show you the way some of the people we think look exciting today put it together for themselves. Your look might be a $2.98 T-shirt with $4.00 strapped canvas shoes from Woolworth's, or maybe it's the day you stun the office with your St. Laurent blazer and $100 rodeo boots, but your look should be in harmony with the way you live, who you are, and not reflect what the fashion magazines (or even we) might say.

The basic concept of Cheap Chic for both men and women is to have a few clothes that make you feel good rather than a closet full of mismatched fashions. Find the clothes that suit you best, that make you feel comfortable, confident, sexy, good looking and happy…and then hang onto them like old friends.

We've become spoiled in America. Surrounded by mass manufacturing and mass marketing, we stuff our closets with masses of mistakes. Fashion seduces us from Sears to Sak's in a dizzying array of styles, prices, fabrics, and colors. We end up with far too many clothes, without stopping to consciously work out our own personal style and gather together the basic elements we need to get it going.

Looking good makes you feel good. Paring down your wardrobe is going to simplify your life. Start dressing to please yourself, and in the process you will please others.

We've divided this book into what looks to us to be the main strata of good dressing in the seventies. We start with "First Layers" which shows how to get maximum mileage from a simple, well-planned wardrobe. The next two sections concern the "Classics" —clothes that have proven themselves timeless, worth the substantial investment because they never disappoint you. Then we take you into antique shops and thrift stores where the good looker can get good looking for very little money and have a lot of fun doing it. "Sports" and "Ethnic" clothes can really add spice and reveal different facets of your personality. "Wrapping" means rock-bottom basics—your body, a bolt of cloth and the imaginative ways one can complement the other. Good old "Work Clothes" are showing up in the smartest places these days, and you'll see why after you look at our 13-button sailor pants that cost less than $10.00. Finally, we conclude with some tips on mixing it all together, caring for the clothes you've come to love and shopping around the world.

The most basic element of Cheap Chic is the body you hang your clothes on. Building a healthy, lively body is far cheaper than buying a lot of clothes to distract from it. And once you really know your flesh and bones, you'll find it easier to choose the clothes you really need and love.

Try standing in front of a full-length mirror some morning, not holding in your stomach, tightening your buttocks, or sticking out your chest. Take a look at your body—front, side, and back. Are you content with what you see? Is your skin clear and healthy? Could the muscle tone of your stomach, upper arms, and thighs be firmed up with a little jogging, swimming, or a ten-block walk each morning? It isn't important if your breasts, hips, or legs aren't those you would see in a fashion magazine or in the pages of *Playboy*. What matters is that you get acquainted with them as they are and treat them with care and respect.

There are no secret recipes for keeping your body together, but learning to take a certain pleasure in self-discipline is a first step… discipline in eating and sleeping habits that helps build good emotional and physical relationships. Once you decide to perk up your body, there are many ways to go about it: Invent your own exercises and treatments, seek advice from a friend who enjoys and studies physical movement, find a class you like, read body books, and keep trying different ways until you find a routine that really feels comfortable for you…one you can really stick with. Diana Vreeland, after almost forty years with *Harper's Bazaar* and *Vogue*, describes the secrets of a vibrant woman: "You have to have a sense of pleasure and a sense of discipline to look really well. You have to have a sound, athletic body, lead a busy life, and worry less. Live correctly and take risks."

Once you have a body program set up, start having fun with your clothes. Perhaps the best place to start thinking about the evocative nature of fabric, color, and clothes is with the senses:

Touch: the softness of washed cottons, thick velvets, tender cashmeres, bumpy corduroys; the harshness of raw wool.

Smell: the scent of a real leather bag versus imitation leather; a wet wool sweater versus a polyester knit.

Sound: the rustle of taffeta, the squawk of rubbers in the rain, the flapping of canvas, the whisper of nylons.

Sight: the harmonious blends of bright or subtle colors, rough and smooth textures, straight and curved silhouettes.

Now, with all your senses in full gear, let's take a look into the world of Cheap Chic.

FIRST LAYERS

There's one very good reason for stocking up on the basics: peace of mind. You'll *never* have to get up in the early morning darkness and stumble about looking for something to match up with something else. If you've got the basics, they're all interchangeable—T-shirts, turtlenecks, or cotton shirts; and with them several pair of jeans, green GI pants, white pants, and a wide skirt. It's rather like wearing a second skin, but more colorful! The reassuring thing about having a drawerful of these things is that you can stick any top with any bottom and it will look great. How can you miss with solid colors, basic quality, simple cut and time-tested designs? And what feels better than slipping into a freshly laundered cotton outfit in your favorite color, tying on a scarf, and giving it no more thought? If you hate to think about what you're putting on your back, and refuse to spend any time messing about with your "wardrobe," you're all set with the basics. You'll have all the more time to get down to what you really want to achieve in life rather than spending hours shopping in department stores and dressing up in a "fashion statement" or a "look for fall." In the basics, you can remain anonymous, observe and stalk the life you're after in a quiet and individual style.

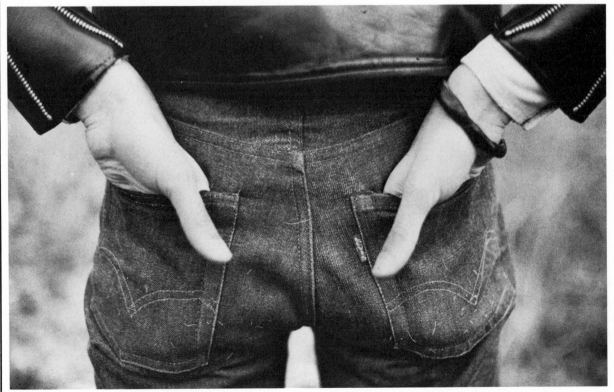

JEANS AND OTHER COVERINGS

One good friend of ours who dresses like a modern-day John Wayne professes to care nothing, or very little, about the clothes he wears. And yet he combs the city to find the precise pair of **jeans** he wants—Lees. Why? Because jeans, like almost everything else, have fallen prey to the fashion cycle. You can find bell-bottomed jeans, boot-leg jeans, even flared jeans. But just try to find a regular, trusty old pair of straight-legged denim jeans with no frills. Our friend has looked in Columbus, Ohio (Surely the farmers would have them!), in Chicago, Illinois, and in Binghamton, New York. His only dependable source: Kauffman's Riding Store in New York City. Jeans are such a totem of American culture that they inspire that kind of mania for the marginal differences, for the tiny details that will set you off from the crowd, set you apart from the blue-legged masses.

In the fifties, jeans were good as gold behind the Iron Curtain: to the Russians they summed up all the romantic promise of the American frontier, the wildness of the West. Like nylons in World War II, jeans were great for bartering and bribing. The Levi trademark—that little red tab sewn into the side of the back pocket—is registered in sixty countries including Russia, where they don't even make jeans.

**Denim Art:
Bill Shire in his
award-winning Levi-
Strauss super-studded
jacket . . . complete with a
built-in ashtray
on the sleeve.**

Forty-Niners at the Last Chance Mine, 1882, wearing riveted Levi's and sturdy boots that look like today's Frye boots.

Originally, jeans were coveted in Paris, and then Yves St. Laurent came along and knocked them off in couture. The French have taken the basic idea of blue jeans, re-styled and recut them for that tight European fit . . . and now they sell like crazy in America at twice the original price. It's typical of the French to pick up basic American design and transform it with colorings and proportion into something quintessentially Parisian, something almost like a national uniform.

A good basic pair of jeans will last several years, mold themselves to your body, and fade with style. Like all good clothes,

Cher, wearing a pair of jeans that fit the way jeans should fit.

they improve with age. In the summer, you can cut them off into shorts; in the winter, open the seams of the legs, set in a piece of denim, and have a warm, long skirt.

The price of jeans is going up, due to world-wide demand for denim, but they remain one of the central American classics.

Once you find a brand of jeans that fits you the way you like to be fit, stick with it. Plan on the waist and inseam shrinking about 8 percent. Levi-Strauss boot-leg jeans are cut shorter in the front of the leg and longer in the back so they'll look good over Frye boots, cowboy boots, or any boots with

16

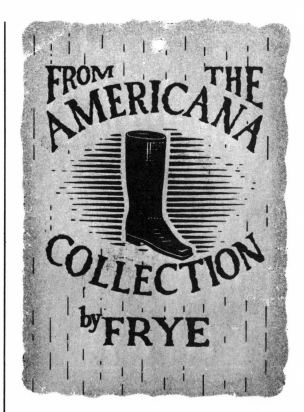

FROM THE AMERICANA COLLECTION by FRYE

heels. Straight-legged Lees have an easy fit and fly front, whereas Wranglers come in a more malleable denim that takes less breaking-in but is less durable. You can choose a less sturdy, less expensive brand like Wayfarers or Landlubbers, which don't last a lifetime but are easily settled into. Once you've settled on your best size and brand, it's sometimes easier to buy them already worn at a swap meet rather than breaking them in yourself. Or, as John Burks noted in a book about jeans, "When you're rich you have them pre-bleached and pressed. Bleached Levi's: upward mobility."

Jeans come in all styles and colors these days, but beware! Stick with straight legs or pegged legs without cuffs, and avoid jeans cut very low on the hips. Even jeans can do you in with supermarket overchoice. Stick to the basics because that "fashion detailing," like industrial-zipper-fly fronts, is going to tire real fast.

If you've never been fond of jeans, consider buying a few pair of green **Army fatigue pants** with the pockets on the sides. All over Europe, fashionable girls are wearing them tucked into the tops of their high leather boots or with a pair of patterned socks and loafers. The fabric is the best, and the U.S. Army is easily the equal of the

Levi-Strauss Company when it comes to putting together a totally functional, beautifully designed piece of clothing.

If you don't relish the thought of marching around looking like a Vietnam vet in jungle green pants, there's yet another alternative—white pants. You can buy white jeans, English or American sailor pants, or painter's pants.

Sailor pants have wide, straight legs and come in a tightly woven long-lasting cotton twill with buttoned closings. They should run about $6 if they're truly "surplus" and not some slyly manufactured imitation. And if they are the real thing, you'll find they take dye beautifully because of their pure cotton fiber.

The first time we saw white **painter's pants** was in a "street fashion" photograph in the Los Angeles *Times*. You can find them at Standard Brands Paints in Los Angeles for 69¢, or in boutiques for several times that. They're a great buy, with all

Twenty years ago
James Dean
seemed stylishly alienated in well-worn denim jeans and a tattered cotton shirt. Today, jeans still have a whiff of the rebel about them ... not without cause.

sorts of mysterious pockets, straps, and tabs designed for the house-painter's craft. A designer in North Hollywood, who could choose to wear any of her luxurious designs, seems to wear nothing but painter's pants and T-shirts under her forties-look velour jackets and coats.

Of course, now that everyone's been wearing pants as a daily routine, there's a strong feeling in the air for **skirts.** We're over the boring, burning issue of how long a skirt should be, and can lean back and

realize how really nice they feel on the legs and how charming they look to others. A tight skirt isn't really practical in this era of constant movement, but an A-line or wrap-around skirt is surely a basic. If you feel your legs are too big for pants, but love

Designer Ola Hudson puts scissors, pins, markers and measuring tapes in the pockets of her sturdy white painter's pants and rotates different long-sleeved cotton T-shirts. With a drawer full of pants and T-shirts, she never has to worry about what to wear to work in the morning.

Peter Hujar's uniform: jeans, an army-surplus leather belt, and a crocodile shirt (without the crocodile).

18

Lauren Hutton's favorite style: jeans, a roomy man's shirt and a pastel Shetland sweater.

the look of jeans, you can get yourself a pocketed, button-front denim skirt or a skirt made of recycled jeans that has the same good qualities you'd find in a pair of jeans—classic looks and durability. In the summer, a loose cotton skirt with a drawstring waist or a full-circle skirt feels airy and sensual and much freer than jeans.

COTTON T-SHIRTS AND OTHER WONDERS

The cheapest mate for your jeans and skirts is a plain cotton T-shirt, so be sure to keep a good supply. A T-shirt in solid colors and different styles can take you through all the seasons. Once you've got a few in your drawer, you'll see how useful and dependable they are.

When you do find your favorite T-shirt, be sure to buy several. Cheap chic doesn't necessarily mean really cheap—spend your money when you find the best style for you.

Buy in multiples, because this is one situation where less is not more. With five perfect T-shirts and three pair of perfectly fitting pants, you ought to stay happily clothed for quite a while.

There is the **cheap, short-sleeved T-shirt** or the undershirt-style T-shirt that comes in white and pastels from discount and dime stores. Often you can find three packaged for $4.98. If they are dyed they look terrific (a dusty rose, for instance, tucked into tight olive pants and high boots). The pastels, like pale sky blue and sunny yellow, are fresh clean colors for summer: they look fine as a skinny-minny T-shirt at the beach. There's nothing like a fresh pastel cotton T-shirt and a warm, mellow touch of sun to make you feel great.

One way to wear these freshly dyed $2 T-shirts is like New York's Puerto Rican kids do in Central Park in the summer: the girls buy extralarge sizes, grab a handful of fabric on either side of the chest, pull it supertight, and make a knot in the front, along the lines of a calypso shirt bodice. It

20   **A T-shirt, with a touch of lace at the neck, dresses up a softly gathered skirt.**

To dye your T-shirt, try Andrea Quinn's recipes with Rit dyes for smokier, sun-bleached colors:
• Burnt Orange: ¼ teaspoon each of Golden Yellow, Orange, Chestnut Brown, and Dark Brown.
• Plum: 1 teaspoon Wine, ¼ teaspoon Charcoal Grey, and ¼ teaspoon Cocoa Brown.
• Fuzzy Green: ½ teaspoon Dark Green and ½ teaspoon Charcoal Grey.
• Blue Smoke: generous ½ teaspoon Navy Blue and skimpy ½ teaspoon Charcoal Grey.
• Mocha Chocolate: generous ½ teaspoon Pink and skimpy ½ teaspoon Dark Brown.

To dye a clean white cotton T-shirt, put on a pair of rubber gloves, line a hand strainer with a paper towel, and put in the dye mix. Hold it under the faucet while you fill the sink with your hottest water, and mix up the water to help it all dissolve. (Undissolved bits of

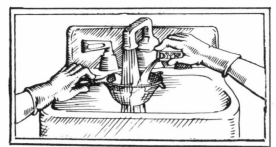

dye will spot your T-shirt.) Then put in a completely wet, clean T-shirt until it turns several shades darker than you want it. It will dry to the color you like (hopefully). The tiny undershirt bows take color faster so dye them separately.

If it comes out a color you don't like, buy some dye remover or stick it back in the basin for a darker color. You can also play with the mix of colors in the shade. To experiment with any colors, mix drops of dissolved dye in a bowl and test the shade with a white paper towel. To dye a skirt or white sailor pants to a matching shade, experiment to find the dye intensity that takes best on that particular fabric.

After you've finished dyeing, dip the clothing into half a cup of vinegar in a sinkful of cold water so the color won't fade. Always wash home-done dye jobs in cold water with a mild soap.

makes for a very narrow, high, tight bust. Cheap Chic! A man's large T-shirt also makes a soft dress to wear at a summer place over a bikini; they even come in handy as swimsuits when you've forgotten yours. Worn over a pair of brightly printed under-

Paul Newman didn't have to dye his undershirt to look like a real peach.

pants or Woolworth's brown $1 "string" bikini, a wet T-shirt can be terribly revealing while protecting you from the sun.

Sometimes you just can't get away with Woolworth's T-shirts, no matter how beautifully they are colored and camouflaged. And it's often very difficult to find plain T-shirts, either long- or short-sleeved. You can buy them with daisies on the front or a laughing cow, or in chartreuse and fuschia stripes; but start looking for a plain, solid color, well-made cotton version. We once spent three hours doing just that in Chicago. And though it may be discouraging, the only plain T-shirt we came up with was a $12 French model at Jax. But since it came

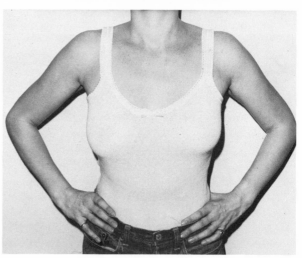

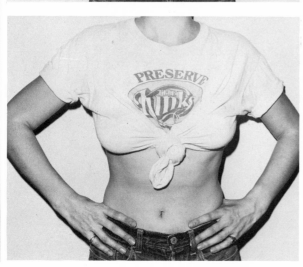

in the style we wanted—completely simple—and in any of twenty-three colors, it was worth the cost. In London you can find the almost impossible item, a basic **long-sleeved T-shirt.** The Biba store carries them. Their resident stylist has a sketchbook full of designing tricks to keep on making them desirable year in and year out. There are scoop necks, square necks, V necks, low-cut necks, all sorts of softened colors, and a cotton knit that only gets better with the years. You can't try them on, but it helps to know that their small, medium, and large run a bit tighter than ours. If a friend goes to London, ask her to stock up for you. They're very cheap.

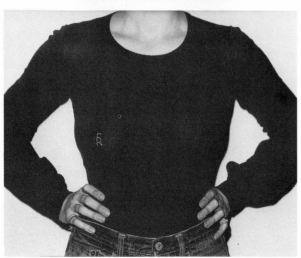

Ingrid Boulting skips rope in Central Park and then bikes to lunch in her plain black T-shirt and pants.

In America you have to spend some time tracking down a store that sells a good basic T-shirt in your city. Luckily, Betsey Johnson is designing an entire group of simple, inexpensive top-and-bottom T-shirt dressings for Tric-Trac that is being manufactured in Morocco to be sold in department stores and shops all over the United States. The pieces and colors are all interchangeable.

When it gets chilly, **turtlenecks** are warmer than the basic T-shirt design. Army-surplus stores carry cheap long-sleeved turtlenecks in cotton knits, but they tend to bag, and sometimes the elastic in the cuffs and neck starts to give and curls out of the cotton knit like little worms after a morning rain.

A really sturdy turtleneck is more expensive, perhaps $15, and comes in a stretchy synthetic mix like nylon and Lycra. These fit beautifully, and the neck never gets worn out from all that on-and-off stretching. They're worth the price, but be sure to get bound seams for your money. When they reach the end of their life, synthetics start to run at the seams, but this isn't for several years of almost daily wearing. A black T-shirt or turtleneck with a pair of black pants can take you almost anyplace, from jogging in the park to dinner at the finest restaurants.

When you're traveling, be sure to pick up a few **tourist T-shirts** for the folks back home. You can find the flashiest styles in the large discount stores of Florida, California, New York, and points between. They have a certain naive exuberance, with their Day-Glo oranges, state maps, and Hollywood fantasies, and they're always made up in cotton. Friends can wear them under or over other T-shirts, or throw out their old pajamas and sleep in a "Florida Sunshine State." A collection of twenty is more than enough to take a person through three changes a day for a week before hitting the washing machine.

For **dress-up T-shirts,** you can transform a scoop neck into a décolleté by gathering the front into a barette-shaped pin between the breasts. Or if you want to really get "steppy" (that's midwestern for fit to kill), buy some cheap, tattered twenties chemises or nightgowns at a thrift shop. You're looking for the lace edgings or beautifully worked pockets. Cut them loose from their old moorings and reapply them to your new T-shirt. With a pair of dusty blue sailor pants dyed to match the top, you've got a fairly delicate evening effect. Or you can stitch on an old piece of fabric or sew a few scarves around the hem of your T-shirt to create a loose and floaty dress.

We're not going to suggest you equip yourself with an embroidery outfit and start some five-hour home project with jeans and T-shirts. We're not getting into crafts, because the idea of Cheap Chic is to save on both the money and the time you invest. We figure that anyone who's sharp enough to buy this book isn't sitting around spending huge amounts of their time "saving money" with homey handiworks when they could be out making the money to save them the time. (Make the money, buy yourself time. *Then* you can dawdle with crafts to your heart's content!)

Popsicle weather clothes:
interchangeable pants, shirts and tops.
Sailor pants with a skimpy cotton top;
a cheap cotton undershirt knotted at
the bust with cigarette-leg jeans; a
military shirt tied at the waist over
straight-legged poplin pants.

LEOTARDS
AND OTHER STRETCHY THINGS

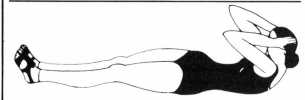

Leotards come in a close second to T-shirts for all-around wearability. They are lightweight, durable, crushproof, quick drying, and they really shape themselves to your body, giving a custom fit at noncustom prices.

A leotard can go under all your basic pants, shirts, and skirts. You can perk it up with a cheap cotton scarf. You can wear it by itself for dancing, exercise, and swimming. And you can pick one up just about anywhere—hosiery shops, dime stores, department stores. Sometimes you can even find a leotard on a rack next to the fruit stand in the supermarket.

A tiny nylon leotard can fit in your pocket for the first ray of sunshine and then take you off to a patch of grass or the seashore. In the summertime, leotards litter the streets of Manhattan . . . its gardens, fire

Capezio makes leotards for professionals . . . and for you.

A few stitches of embroidery on a leotard becomes an incentive for exercising.

escapes, and six-by-nine terraces. From Montauk to Malibu Beach, limbs and spines stretch and shimmy in these little pieces of nylon.

Danskin is one of the best leotard makers. Like Levi-Strauss, they've been in their

The infinite variety of classic cotton shirts: full-bodied and full-sleeved; gathered at the yoke or tight to the body; generously wrinkled or finely pressed. Wear a big shirt over a tiny bandeau or halter and it becomes a jacket; wear it over a bikini and it's an instant beach dress.

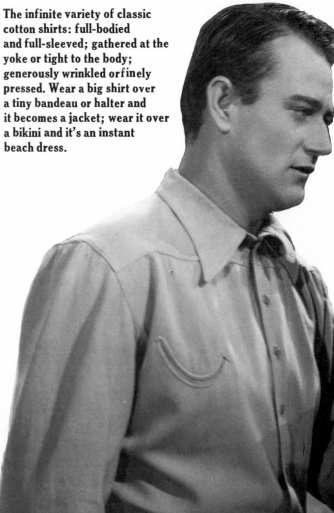

Worn over a turtleneck, a shirt can double as a jacket.

Try unbuttoning your shirt to the waist, like a swash-buckling version of Errol Flynn.

exercise class. (One small warning: Keep an eye on your layering when you wear a leotard without a snap crotch. The snapless leotards are smoother and healthier, but it takes forever to unpeel yourself in the bathroom!)

If you don't feel comfortable in skin-tight turtlenecks and T-shirts and leotards, gather up a collection of **loose cotton shirts.** A man's old shirt can look terrific tucked in at the waist over a turtleneck; or, if it's large and straight at the bottom, pulled tight with a wide belt at the waist. If the collar has seen better days, cut it off above the seam where it joins the shirt, turn it under, and sew into place. If the shirttails are too curved, cut them straight and then hem them. A lot of women sneak into the boy's department of Brooks Brothers, the crusty old men's outfitters in New York. When the owners found they were buying boy's shirts to wear, they made one conces-

business a long time and are extremely knowledgeable in the ways of manufacturing a long-lasting, durable product. The locked seams hold together under the stretchiest of stretches. And they come in a great variety of shapes and colors. A recent classic is the Capezio wraparound skirt dyed to match their leotards, perfect for business travel and trips to and from an

30 | **Helene Gaillet's self-portrait: The real first layer is a lithe, supple body.**

sion: they made up a cotton broadcloth button-down shirt sized for women. But for some reason, the boy's shirts are as popular as ever, perhaps because of that loose, low-arm-holed look and those pure cottons you'd pay four times as much for in other stores (if you could find them). And you can order them easily by mail.

So choose your skirts, pants, and tops very carefully. Now, sit back and relax. You can stop reading this book right here, and if you happen to live in a warm climate, you'll have enough clothes to take you through the whole year.

THE LAYER ESCALATION

One woman who has made a total discipline out of dressing around the basics is Helene Gaillet, a New York photojournalist. Her working day usually starts at eight sharp and keeps her running until six or often seven at night. Since she has little time to change from working clothes to evening clothes, she's eliminated dress-up clothes as much as possible from her wardrobe. She works at such an intense pitch that she has to be very careful about keeping both her body and her clothes in perfect running order. Her clothes are now so few and so honed down that when she travels, she takes only one duffel bag, which fits under the airplane seat in front of her. Here are her rules.

This gold and leather English cavalry belt has been worn with jeans every other day for over ten years and it looks better now than ever.

The monogrammed boy's shirt is a basic element in Helene Gaillet's special system of year-round layering.

"Ninety-five percent of my clothes are in navy blue, white, or khaki. I never go shopping, and when I do, I know specifically what I want. I have an $80 or $100 bill a year plus shoes, and that's it.

"I buy my jeans in shades of blue at the army-navy store. They're always Levi's, often in corduroy. The Levi cut is thinner—they seem to cut Wranglers for big asses and Levi's for almost nonexistent asses! Levi's are cut straight and never need to be tailored to fit me.

"I wear the same shirt all year round, even when I'm skiing. It's the layer theory: one, two, three, or four things go on top of each other. My cotton turtlenecks go under the shirt—they're $3 at the army-navy store, or $10 in an imported stretch acrylic fabric. I get the little-boy's button-down oxford shirt from Brooks Brothers in three colors—white, the blue stripe, and yellow—a dozen at a time every three years. They're $7 plus $2 for the initials, and that way it looks

An inexpensive shirt, jeans, a belt and overshirt are complemented by Helene's collection of gold jewelry.

one or two pair a year and wear them over three or four years. They're usually English or French. My pant boots are $60 from Veneziano, but I usually buy St. Laurent boots; one pair long, the other short to go under jeans, and they run around $100 a pair. I've found the trick to keeping jeans tucked into your boots—fit a pair of bright red 69¢ socks from Woolworth's over your pant legs with tights underneath. I love wearing bright red underthings!

"To go with the tops and jeans, I have just three belts that I bought in the sixties: an old leather army belt from the flea market in Paris, a Turkish metal belt from an antique store, and a gold-and-leather English cavalry belt from the Chelsea Antique Market that I wear about every other day. They were all under $20.

"My everyday winter outfit is my jeans, turtleneck, shirt, and T-shirt, plus a fisherman's sweater from the Fulton Street Fish Market, a belt, and usually a long, thrift-shop scarf. If it's really cold, I add a $6 safari jacket from the army-navy store. And

like you're wearing a $30 custom shirt. Then I have three good silk shirts, all in ivory white. My oldest one is eight years . . . I got it on sale for $50. But they usually only last two or three years, because they get yellowish with dry cleaning.

"Boots are one of my most expensive items because I literally live in them. I get

The ins-and-outs of the over-and-under school of dressing: Helene puts on a T-shirt, a boy's shirt, a denim overshirt, tucks it all into jeans and a pair of good leather boots and then relaxes.

always boots, a canvas camera bag (actually a game bag, which was a gift, because I think they're too expensive), a $2 denim hat from the dime store, and a pair of sunglasses.

"In the summer I wear cutoffs, Cloroxed $6 Wayfarer jeans, and T-shirts I can throw in the washing machine. If it gets cold, I put on a denim shirt.

"I just don't buy expensive things, except boots."

"For evening wear, I've worked out a 'tuxedo'—eight-year-old wool gabardine St. Laurent pants copied by Alexander's department store with a black velvet jacket from a boutique, plus a vest and cheap satin shirt. I wear it with strapped sandals and flaming red tights, and the red toes peek out from under all the black!

"I do sink money in accessories: I always wear the same ones, and I do spend on them. I've got a five-year-old brown suede pouch from La Bagagerie. All my gold things have been stolen twice, so I don't have much left: five rings, a Cartier tank watch with a clasp that cost $600 in Paris eight years ago, a Van Cleef and Arpels bracelet, and some gold chains. They're like good-luck charms. I even swim and sleep with them on.

"In the last year I've gone from 124 pounds to around 118 at five foot six. My secret is a small breakfast: a glass of orange juice, four cups of very strong espresso, and a toasted English muffin. I eat lunch less than once a week, and when I do, try to make it Japanese. And then I eat anything for dinner, but very little. That way I never diet!

"I go to an exercise class twice a week. I spend my money there and on having my hair streaked. And I've done the Royal Canadian Air Force exercises ten minutes every morning since 1962. I save money on cabs by doing everything on my bike or on foot; and year round I play tennis and ski. I'd love to be one of the great beauties, but, to make the best of myself, I have to radiate what I can get from inside: health. I think your mental attitude is based on your physical well-being."

Winterize the layered look with a navy sweater, a safari jacket, high boots and a hat.

RUDI GERNREICH

From Body Clothes to Uniforms

Rudi Gernreich is a wizard at sensing social trends and designing one step ahead of them. Rudi gained worldwide fame for the topless bathing suit and lately the Thong. But his real impact has come from popularizing simple, stretchy, revealing body clothes.

Rudi was born in Vienna, where his father was a hosiery manufacturer. The family fled Austria in 1938 and settled in Los Angeles when Rudi was sixteen. He studied art, became a modern dancer for ten years, then went into swimsuit design. Now he's done it all. He was the first to bring out the maillot, an unconstructed knitted tank suit, and body awareness was born. Women could no longer camouflage and pad their bodies. His topless suit in 1964 led to the No-Bra and the body stocking. In the sixties Rudi designed for the feeling of greater freedom and exposure for the body. He was right. He sees impersonal uniforms in the future.

Rudi's spacious office in Los Angeles has a floor of cool white tiles, a two-story ceiling, large plants, a glass table, zebra rug, four chairs, two couches, and one white cube.

"I think people either have style or they don't, regardless of what it costs. Whatever they do will have style.

"For the future, I see very functional clothes. Not just for economy—to be nonconspicuous in public. People won't want to attract attention to themselves, so they won't be attacked. And not just physically, but psychologically. Poor people are constantly exposed to a better life through TV, and it makes them angry. So there will be this trend toward wearing uniforms, unisex clothes.

"In the interim period, people will want to relieve the austerity in their private environment. They'll want things that relate to tasteful people's value systems . . . there will be much more of a show of imagination. They'll be much freer with private surroundings, but they'll move away from the focus on the self to a focus on the surroundings. Twenty years ago, you could find a very tastefully dressed woman, and you couldn't believe her house. Her focus was only on herself, not on the objects surrounding her. But in the future, a person will have to create a better environment and be selective with friends.

"There is a greater awareness today with young people of how they take care of themselves. Jeans have become the new uniform, the number-one part of the wardrobe. I wear body clothes—like a black leotard body shirt and blue pants. You can wear body clothes successfully with exercise. They're unisex, but people misunderstand unisex. If a man wears something it becomes male; a woman, female. I've done a new form of body wear for Lily of France in Lycra. I think stretch knits in light weights are the most legitimate use of synthetics. Otherwise I use muslin, chambrays, denims, and pure cotton.

"In the future there will not be any more of the pure fabrics, because labor all over the world is changing. It takes slave labor to get that kind of quality. In twenty years, people will not even understand what that quality is.

"In America, there's still too much uptightness about how you should dress. In

the sixties you had to have 'a wardrobe of swimsuits.' You'd take ten with you on a weekend. All you need is two. One to wear, one to dry. And it's still deeply believed that you have to have five pair of pants, a ward-robe that says 'Good Living and Affluence.' It's been pounded into your head that be-cause of America's overproduction ethic it's unthinkable for someone to have just one pair of pants. Perhaps that's all you need."

CLASSICS

Sometimes Cheap Chic boils down to spending much more than you feel you can afford on the kind of classic, quality clothes we talk about in this chapter. We think it saves you money in the long run. If you're a real purist, Cheap Chic can become a matter of extremes: throwing your last $150 into a tweed riding jacket and riding out poverty in style. But if you don't feel comfortable investing in truly expensive classics, then consider buying some of the second-string classics we'll be talking about in the next chapter, like a lovely Shetland sweater or cowboy boots.

There are still certain things you shouldn't fudge on no matter how cheaply you dress: the very best boots, a sturdy bag, a glorious jacket or shirt. You can't afford cheap boots that will last a year and then crack across the sole. If you had loads of money you could; but since you don't, spend your money where it shows the most.

If you look closely at a woman with a strong individual style, you will discover there is almost always something in her outfit that costs a lot. Perhaps it's a five-year-old pair of French boots or a simple, solid-gold chain around her wrist. Whatever it is, that one touch makes her look ten times better. The throwaway chic gives her an intriguing look.

It might seem impossible to think of yourself laying out $100 on a pair of boots. If so, start saving, even if it's only $5 a week. If you can't manage that, then stop smoking, and start eating soybean protein! In five years you'll still be wearing those boots (inflation will then have jacked them up to $300) and they will look beautifully, aristocratically worn and weathered. They'll save

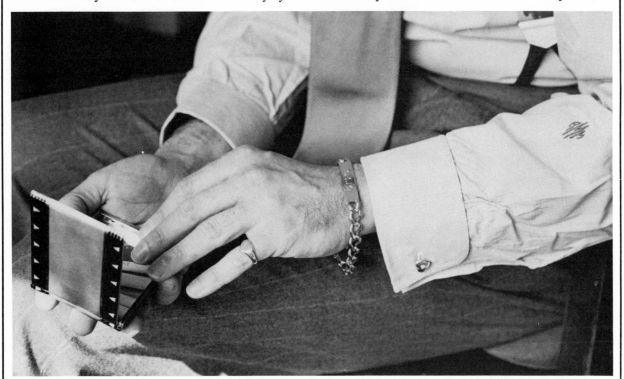

A well tailored suit can last decades. Antonio Lopez's suit is made of black cashmere by Cifonelli in Paris.

your wardrobe with a cheeky touch of class even when you're really hard up and down to your last pair of jeans.

This is a very European way of dressing. French designer Emmanuelle Khanh thinks that the great thing about France is the *bon gout*, the good taste. "It's a process of refining that's been going on for centuries. We're more moderate and appreciate quality, so our clothes last longer. Since we don't exaggerate our appearance, we have more balance in choosing our personal styles. At first it may look as if we're wearing a uniform, but then you notice the subtle differences in shades, cuts, and quality of fabric. An older woman is often seen in what a girl of eighteen buys because it's all based on classic proportion."

You can keep a very small closet if you're careful, almost ruthless, in choosing your few classic investments. Tina Bossidy, a nine-to-five fashion editor in New York, has it down to a system. She believes in that old fashion-magazine idea of "setting up a wardrobe." It sounds terribly stuffy, because we haven't needed the discipline to think this way for a long time. But the results can be great—a group of clothes that are not faddy, that are not going to pass out of style, and that you can build up year after year. What this plan involves, again, is a much smaller, more thought-out wardrobe. Here are some of her tips.

• **Color** is the most important thing in dressing well. The whole point of looking good is feeling good, so find the colors that make you feel best and stick with them. Women often forget they look very good in soft colors, like a light turquoise. Try it.

• One of the big mistakes is buying **prints.** If you develop your sense of color and buy mainly solids, everything will work together.

• A big secret is to buy things in **multiples.** Once you find your favorite colors, the easiest thing to do is to set up a sort of *uniform* of top quality: For instance, buy six mens' silk shirts when they go on sale: blue, red, black, green, maroon, turquoise, and purple. Buy two identical skirts: purple and black. Department stores usually overbuy. If something falls into the uniform category, then it will probably go on sale in three weeks to a month, even at the designer boutiques. Then, if you can afford it, buy two good coats and two good jackets, since that's what you're seen in first.

• Supplement these investments with thirteen-button navy wool pants, cotton and velour pullovers, T-shirts, and cotton drawstring pants.

• Shoes and boots are some of the most important things you can have in your wardrobe. Spend money on styles like short pink boots cuffed at the top, brandy kidskin boots, ponyskin pumps—things that really set you off.

• All other shopping can be done from thrift shops and army surplus—here's where

you find your basics and special accessories, lots of bright belts, and jewelry.

The color, the quality, and the limited quantity of this wardrobe give you a luxurious style on a tight budget. Special accessories raise it from the rank of a working-woman's uniform.

You're always going to get the most out of your money by buying something really luxurious that makes you feel fantastic, wearing it to death, and paying absolutely rock bottom for the cheap things you can get away with. Draw the line at quality; don't skimp on the classics. And in ten years, who knows? You might even have an air of shabby gentility! Classics are clothes that last.

Ching dresses down his black cashmere sweater with suspendered jeans while Sibao looks traditionally discreet.

40

ACCESSORIES

Sink your money into a very good pair of **boots.** Expensive European boots are a consistent favorite among snappy dressers who spend their money sparingly but buy things that last. You'll often find a pair of four-year-old St. Laurent boots making a very cheap turnout look terribly chic. It's not because they bear the name St. Laurent, though he does have a first-rate sense of classic design. It's because they're made in a European

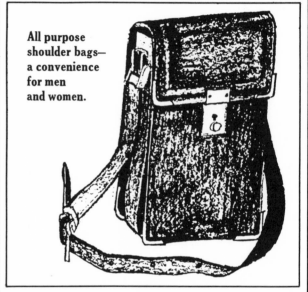

All purpose shoulder bags— a convenience for men and women.

artisan tradition with good lasts, hand finishing, the best leathers, and sumptuous colors.

Boots not only look good, they feel good. How far and how fast can you walk in a pair of high-heeled pumps? Boots look just as good, and you can really walk your heart out in them. The money you save on cabs and buses will pay for the next pair. But a European last is uncomfortable for some American feet, so never talk yourself into a pair of good boots unless they fit perfectly. A seamstress can do nothing about this particular problem!

Although it's perfectly sensible to buy black or brown, some girls go out and find just one pair of the very best boots in colors like gray, red, green, or burgundy. They figure it looks like you have lots more at home. So if acid green cheers you up, why not acid green?

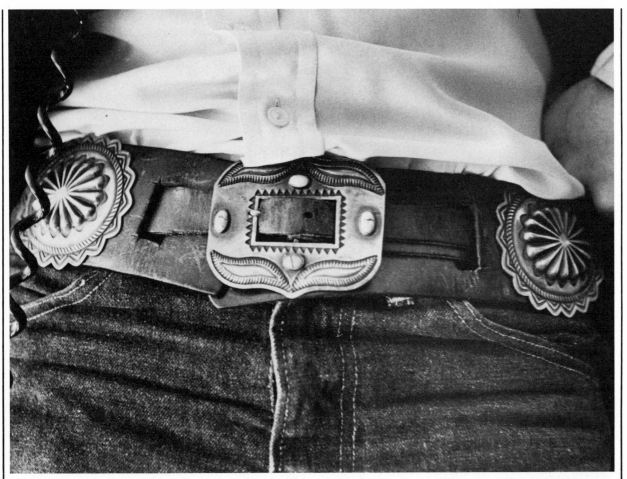

A real investment, the concho belt is worth its price in good silver and fine turquoise. Its value grows with age.

The best quality, quietly conservative **men's shoes** can be found in the Brooks Brothers catalog. Peal & Company and the "Brooks English" line have wingtips with very thin soles, not those thick Big Mac numbers most guys walk around on, as well as simple oxfords and rakish tassel loafers. If you want to head for the very best, Lobb Bootmaker's representative takes orders in the spring and fall at a shop called Everall Brothers in New York.

Belts are worth an investment, since they will last a lifetime. A silver belt looks spectacular with anything from a tweed skirt to a pair of skintight leather jeans. Be sure any "investment belt" can fit in both places, at the waist or hip. You can occasionally find antique silver belts from Turkey at street markets and obscure shops, but they usually wend their way to the more pricey boutiques and antique stores. If you buy one of the large silver belts sold by weight, the heavier the better. (You can always hock it.) If you don't like silver, keep your eyes open for that unique, one-of-a-kind belt that looks as if it had always belonged to you, and buy it on the spot.

A good basic leather belt, totally simple, can be worn with interchangeable buckles. The buckles can be your personal trademarks. For about $25 you can buy a fine lizard belt from Tony Lama at a western

**The ultimate in custom –
made shoes are these now forbidden,
handmade, crocodile tasseled
loafers worn by Richard Merkin.**

A touch of gold at the neck often catches a ray of sunlight.

the ounce, closed by a hand-soldered S. A plain gold chain looks perfect at wrist, waist, finger, or neck. Smooth hoops in pierced ears last a lifetime, and a gold band is almost nicer than a diamond. Gold can always be sold or bartered—it's much better than dollars.

If you wear a **watch,** you'll probably be seeing more of that than anything else you own. The nicest watches seem to be the most simple, not too tiny and "feminine," but something with a readable face and the best-quality brown or black leather band you can afford.

Today, the size of your **bag** seems to matter more than variety or expense. It used to be that you could always spot a "lady" by her shoes and purse. But now many of us are walking around in sneakers with portable offices in our purses—address book, note pad, appointment calendar, magazines, some letters, bills, makeup, Instamatic, small electronic calculator, checkbook, and wallet. With all this stuff to cart around, size becomes the primary consideration. The best place to find a sturdy leather or canvas bag is in the luggage department, in sporting goods stores, or at prestigious old-line leathergoods shops like Crouch & Fitz-

store to wear with a big oval silver-and-gold rodeo belt buckle. Steer clear of imitation-antique, imitation-brass buckles, because there are just too many of them around.

A concho belt in silver, turquoise, and worn brown leather is a collector's item, a good investment now that they are no longer at the height of fashion. If you prefer to wear your art around your waist rather than on a wall, here's your chance.

Real jewelry adds a quiet little touch of elegance. Perhaps the most beautiful and inexpensive gold jewelry comes from Thailand—simple, tiny gold chains bought by

| **If you must wear a watch, choose one carefully so it will blend with all of your clothes and still be functional.**

gerald in New York. A leather bag from a department store is going to cost too much: a simple legal-pad-sized shoulder bag is now up to $140, and the Hermès leather shoulder bag is a staggering $600 with tax.

If you can't afford a leather bag, it's awfully luxurious to use a leather-lined canvas bag, if you can find one. Some sly women-about-town buy the $20 Danish schoolbag by mail from Chocolate Soup in

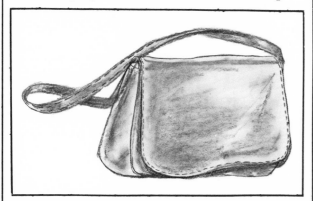

A durable shoulder bag of canvas or leather travels well.

New York and sink the rest of their money into one beautiful, obviously expensive leather accessory like an address book or small monogramed diary from a place like Mark Cross. Whether you choose leather or canvas, it's always nice to have a clutch purse slipped inside for pared-down situations, like a business lunch at a good restaurant.

CLOTHES CLASSICS

Old etiquette books used to list the minimum wardrobe an impoverished gentleman of quality might collect. It is a system of dressing where less is more . . . of necessity! Transposing the rules for a man's wardrobe to a woman's can give you a fresh approach for a well-thought-out closet.

Three or four suits: a brown one, a gray pinstripe, a tweed or tan gabardine, and, in hot climates, a summer seersucker or white linen.

Jackets: One navy blazer and one brownish tweed sport coat.

Two or three pair of pants: gray flannel, beige whipcord, and perhaps white flannel for eccentricity's sake.

Three pair of shoes: brown single-sole wingtips, brown tassel loafers, and perfectly plain black oxfords.

A woman organizing her wardrobe on this minimalist principle would substitute a skirt here and a riding jacket there. Think of the ease with which you could dress. There would be absolutely no room to make a mistake (unless something didn't get back from the cleaner's in time for you to get to work in the morning!). Think of the beautiful, uncommon effect of such understated elegance—especially when mixed in with a few pair of Levi's and shiny boots. A couple of things from the classics lend presence and weight to all the clothes in your closet.

Before we run through some of the classic investments you might want to make, we offer a word of warning: In buying tailored clothes, steer clear of foppish effects like flapped and buttoned pockets, patch

Francois de Menil blends a classic St. Laurent blazer, a silk shirt, Levi's jeans and Lucchese boots from Texas.

pockets, contrasting-color overstitching on lapels, snazzy buttons, inverted pleats, epaulets, and gewgaws of all descriptions. You're going for well-tailored, expensive clothes that will not call attention to themselves and will not look out of fashion in six to eight years. Try to find an old-line conservative tailor whose judgment you can trust. Look at old pictures in movie books and magazines—there really are timeless looks that you can step right into today.

The **blazer** is one of the most elegant yet congenial designs from the classical repertoire. Navy blue is the traditional color; the cut is usually double breasted. If you have a blazer tailor made, it can be lengthened and shortened, made boxier or more shapely, according to the feel of the times. The blazer is ageless.

A black velvet blazer or lush green smoking jacket has become a dinner party classic. Wear it with cowboy boots, jeans, and an old belt. Put a flower at the lapel (gardenias waft deliciously as you walk down the street), put a wisp of silk at the neck or, if

Most classic wardrobes include a calf-length cape, a well fitted wool riding jacket and an all purpose raincoat. Left: Captain Bogart rides the waves in a timeless, navy wool crewneck sweater.

you can't get a fresh flower, make yourself a cluster of satin lingerie flowers from the twenties. And blaze.

If you must have a **suit,** it's best to get one that can go a million different ways—the jacket with jeans, the slacks with shirts and Shetlands. The owner of a men's boutique in New York suggests that a dark blue suit with a vest is the absolute minimum a man can have in his closet (along with a pair of Levi's, a drip-dry shirt, and a silk shirt). Another designer likes a navy serge suit backed up with a chalk pinstripe and a gray flannel—all paired with shirts of the same tone. A Prince of Wales glen plaid suit is the height of daytime elegance but trousers can't live a double life as easily as gray flannel or blue serge, but that's the price you pay for the sublime! Lauren Bacall wears a black, man's tailored suit with a polka-dot silk hankie and fuschia stitching on the lapel buttonhole.

You can dress a **riding jacket** up or down, over a Shetland sweater and jeans, or with a silk shirt and luscious brown velvet skirt.

Greta Garbo knew it all the time—her taste is so classic that she could step out of the 1940s right into the 1970s.

Dietrich's mysterious sexuality changed the tailored look.

The psychology of a riding jacket is fascinating, especially if it has a worldly patina. It seems to demand a stance of being in command, a certain swagger and controlled elegance . . . pure attitude. If it's difficult to find a riding jacket in your area, you can order from one of the riding stores in New York that stock English and French imports, and have it tailored once it arrives.

A good pair of pure wool **slacks** will last years. If you can't afford to have them custom-tailored, you can order something called made-to-measure, put together from a combination of existing patterns. Or you can order by mail from Brooks, Chipp, or Press. Women can find well-cut slacks in boutiques and good department stores. Gray is a good color if you can only afford one pair, as is beige gabardine. Navy blue wool has a very sober and bracing elegance and can take you anywhere. The best cut is very conservative, with small pleats and straight legs. If they start to get shiny, they can be deshined by a special cleaning process listed in the back of this book. Tailor-made slacks

cost little more than very good ones in department stores. If you find the right tailor, you can get them for $50–$80, and have everything exactly as you like it—pockets, watch pocket, cuffs, pleats, belt loops, zipper or button fly.

A **cape** is a necessary accoutrement for swirly, dramatic people. Look for a fluid, loose, ample fabric you can whoosh around in, drape over your arm, or throw over a shoulder like a scarf for the body. The black wool Spanish cape with its high collar is a good buy. The full-length wool Inverness cape from Scotland is especially dashing. And plain old cashmere makes the softest cape of all.

To wrap up the classics in the middle of

Never go anywhere without a trench coat. This is St. Laurent's; Burberry or Brooks Brothers are comparable.

46

a downpour, try a British **trench coat.** The Burberry is more than a raincoat—it can serve as a top layer year round, over a thick sweater in winter and a thin T-shirt in summer showers. The trench coat design is timeless, with its epaulets, knotted belt, slash pockets, and raglan sleeves.

We talk a lot about the **silk shirt.** A good one is hard to find. Some people dislike silk because it tends to feel clammy if you perspire. The secret to wearing a silk shirt is to buy it very loose, so that it is not cut in tightly under the armpits. Then perspiration is able to evaporate off your body and won't stain the armpit. The other problem with silk is that it takes an incredible beating at the cleaners. So the other secret to wearing a silk shirt is learning to wash it gently by hand in lukewarm water and then have it pressed at the cleaner's. Once you master the care and feeding of a silk shirt, there is nothing that will look so luxurious, wear so beautifully, and feel so incredible. Silk picks up everything you own, including your spirits.

Yves St. Laurent makes ample silk shirts in a wide variety of colors. One of his crepe de Chine shirts has full sleeves, a sheared back and front, a narrow collar band, and a front placket. It is soft and loose; the look is elegant lassitude. Tuck it in as a blouson, wear it out as an overshirt, wrap it with a wide leather belt, or knot it over a swirling skirt. Or wear one traditional shirt over another and layer the collars like the petals of a flower.

You can often find a better shirt in the men's line—the cut is bigger, the tails are longer, the stitching is closer. Turnbull & Asser of London will make them up in any shape you prefer for around $125, or in the very finest cotton for less. If you're not ready to spring a week's wages for a shirt, send for samples of the beautiful $6-a-yard crepe de Chine at Oriental Silk in Los Angeles and ask a seamstress to copy a friend's shirt. Or, again, you could be patient and do very well at a half-price sale. Silk shirts that have faded where they've been folded sometimes sell for $25 at St. Laurent (25 percent of their original price) but they need to be dyed a dark color or worn under

Even a plain business suit looked sexy on Bogey.

a sweater so just the collars and cuffs show.

Richard Merkin dresses only in tailored clothes and thinks they are, indeed, heaven incarnate. Every morning Richard gets up in his apartment on New York's West Side, pulls on a battered old gray sweatsuit, and jogs through Riverside Park. When he gets back, he changes into his work clothes and goes into his painter's studio until three in the afternoon. Then, Richard turns toward his vast, overflowing closet and chooses the suit, tie, shirt, collar, suspenders, socks, and shoes for his tailor-made composition of the day. Richard Merkin, artist, becomes Richard Merkin, noted dandy, a man fascinated by dress, and especially by the aristocratic British tailoring which he affects to an extreme. Once you read and absorb Richard Merkin's views, you should be able to talk to any British tailor with ease. Tailor-made clothes are nothing more or less than a collaboration between you and the tailor; part fabric, part psychology. Here's what happens when you develop a craving for the real thing.

Richard Merkin's classic dinner jacket is highlighted by a lavender carnation and a slick shoeshine.

"I started having clothes made for me in the sixties, when my first show of paintings sold out in Boston. Before that I couldn't afford it! My suits from 1964 look as new as a suit I would have made today. But ten years ago, you could get a really good custom suit for $190 . . . now a good custom suit is upwards of $380.

"George Frazier was the most elegant man I've ever known, a columnist and journalist who wrote for *Esquire* and the Boston *Globe*. He didn't have very much clothing, but everything he had was impeccable. There was no room for any mistake. And it wasn't self-conscious, it was at one with him. Every so often I used to wear both a flower and a handkerchief, and George always chided me for it. He said it was disturbing to have put the two things together. He was right. It's just a spot of color that accents a whole totality. And it shouldn't be two spots.

"I like the idea of being able to take a classical form and punctuate it with invention so that you come up with something like a new color combination, or just using an unexpected collar with a suit. Most guys who were concerned dressers in the twenties wore flowers in their lapel. People come up to me and say, 'Where did you get that flower?' It's just a carnation. But the point of it is the concern, of course. I mean, a flower is really beautiful, it's very perfect . . . a beautiful flower and a good shoeshine. Nowadays most ready-made suits have no buttonhole. How sad.

"George Frazier always said, 'Wanna know if a guy is well-dressed? Look down.' The greatest degeneration of any particular garment is shoes. The nicest shoes you can find are those old Brooks Brothers brown ones. Outside of dancing pumps, they're the most elegant. I wear dancing pumps a lot in the summer when I'm not wearing socks. And I love tassel loafers.

"I think we live in a time when people are superficially more interested in dress than they ever have been. People today want approval for the way they dress, which is the kiss of death. You really can't 'do your own thing' unless you know who you are. I think there's a very delicate kind of merger between your clothes and your personality, a give and take between who you are and what you're wearing. When I get dressed, I do become a little bit more severe, more decisive. Actually, I think the most fashionable dressers are the nonfash-

Mr. Merkin, a perfectionist in his attire, likes to accent his grey pinstripe double-breasted suit with a British bowler and butter cotton gloves.

David Croland bought his one dollar tuxedo in a thrift shop, had it recut twice and is determined to have it copied if it doesn't hold up for another five years.

ionable dressers. Style really has to do with being able to perceive what's best for you; taking care to analyze just the way something really looks. For instance, a really big tie doesn't look good on everybody. I can't stand shirts with crippling patterns. You have to be very careful about things like lapels, which can get too big and fall into caricature and trendiness.

"The really great dandies devoted a major section of their life to dressing. Certainly in Beau Brummell's case it didn't lead to ostentation. It led to dressing that was perfect, just absolutely perfect, nothing off, not a hair!

"Obviously, that takes a lot of concern and a lot of time. If you need two hours to dress in the morning and you have to be at work at nine, then you have to get up at seven. Is that approaching insanity? No, it's approaching perfection, but then perfection is just a stone's throw away from insanity.

"I don't understand the passion for informality, the contemporary loathing for discipline. There's an absolute fetish these days about being comfortable, being loose. But I rather like the idea of a starched collar.

It's not as comfortable as an open-neck shirt . . . but it's beautiful looking! Why not put up with a little discomfort to achieve a more significant effect?

"When I say somebody dresses well, I mean cohesively. It doesn't mean just like me. For instance, I'm a fight fan and I've seen some pimp types who were fabulously dressed! Those guys really know what their *body* looks like.

"I'm terribly contrary, and if something becomes popular, it generally gets ruined, and I'll give it up like that! I never wear jeans. And I don't like costume, putting things together for an effect which may not be beautiful and may not have anything to do with your life. I like things that are ordered, the same kind of order I look for in a painting or in a supper or in a girlfriend or in a car . . . a blend of the function and the form of it.

"Art is exactly as important to me as the way I dress. When I choose a tie and a shirt in the morning it's no less important to me than going in and making a picture. It's the same.

"But I am an artist, so I really hate it when I buy a shirt and the guy says 'Would you like a tie to go with that?' It's the 'go with' syndrome. And if somebody puts his name on something, I don't buy it. I'll wear a tailor's name, but a designer's? Any person is a unique totality, and what does St. Laurent know about where I grew up and what I think?

"Unless something is made absolutely right, it bothers me, so I spend the extra money. But if I didn't have any money, I'd much rather go to a thrift shop and find some old English suit or jacket and bring it to a tailor than go buy something off the rack in a department store.

"You see, most people mistrust any kind of classical values or verities. I think there are certain articles of clothing that are absolutely the most impeccable: the summer Panama hat, a black satin tie with a clean knot, a navy blue blazer, the pink Brooks button-down, a double-breasted Chesterfield with a black velvet collar. I mean, all these things are just absolutely the *zenith* of gorgeousness. All you have to do is buy them! There it is!"

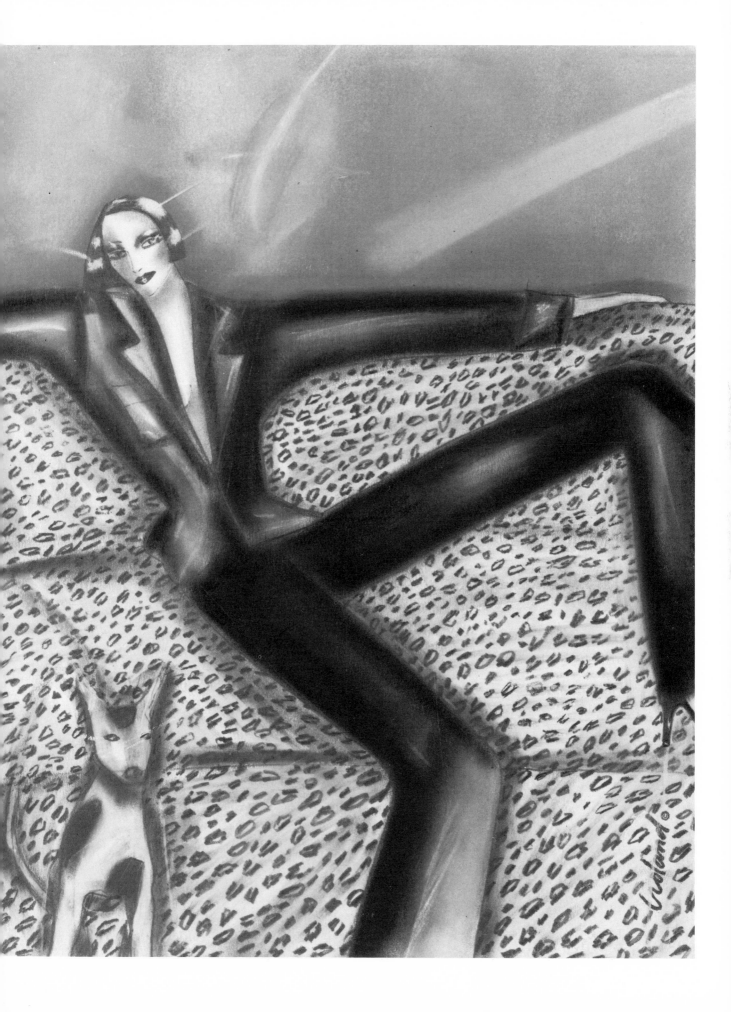

DIANA VREELAND

Eccentric Elegance from the World of Vogue

For more than thirty-five years, Diana Vreeland has been a leading figure in the international world of fashion, first at Harper's Bazaar and then as editor-in-chief at Vogue. *Since October 1972 Mrs. Vreeland has been Special Consultant to the Costume Institute at the Metropolitan Museum of Art in New York. The three exhibitions she has mounted for the museum are "The World of Balenciaga," "Inventive Clothes, 1909–1939," and "Romantic and Glamorous Hollywood Design." The exhibitions have broken attendance records at the museum and exerted a major influence on current fashion and design.*

A woman of great charisma and originality, Diana Vreeland speaks her mind about style, the importance of a fit body, and an element she still exudes in her mid-seventies, energy.

"I think everything is habit. Everything builds on itself. Energy builds on energy like

The super-pros at the Metropolitan's Costume Institute.

love builds on love. Everything intensifies itself. This is habit. Energy and love are good habits, sometimes there are bad habits. Stimulation is happy energy. Then the energy produces itself and your excitement about whatever is going on.

"I think it's a very difficult moment to write a book on fashion. The first thing a girl's got to do is to keep herself together physically with any small amount of money she's got. However she does it, that comes before anything. This is a very vital moment. You have to be very healthy today—your skin, your eyes, your everything.

"Basically, people only look well if they have a very, very good foundation. You know what that means? You can't cover anything up with paint and powder. But I am tired of the natural look. I am fed up to the teeth. God Almighty, some of the girls who come into my office. Oh, how they look! For what is all this natural look? It must be for them, it certainly can't mean

Mrs. Vreeland's classic winter uniform: three black cashmere sweaters rotated with three black Givenchy skirts.

anything to anyone else. I am mad about artificial appearances beautifully done—the gilded lily is irresistible.

"The natural look is too colorless. Don't forget that the white person is not beautiful. Pale skin is not beautiful. It's very rare you see extraordinarily clear white skin. It's usually sallow. We are uneven owing to the many mixtures of bloods. So we've got to build ourselves up to something.

"You have to start with your face and hair and your body. Forget clothes until you've got these basics straight. Once you've got that in hand (if you're young you can do it very quickly), then you get with the clothes. I think clothes come second. Clothes are decor and you've got to have something to put them on. I'm not talking about expensive clothes. I don't see why clothes should be expensive. But don't forget I am talking about a girl with everything absolutely as best as she can do it . . . her hair, her eyes, her strength, her walk, her expression, everything. She's totally with it. That comes before clothes. Men the same. And for children too, but they have it naturally.

"First, I'd put money into shoes. No variety, just something I could wear with everything. Marvelous shoes and boots. Whatever it is you wear, I think shoes are terribly important. My shoe, that strap shoe, I had made again and again for about thirty years. Now I have pumps and boots made exactly as I want them.

"Style is everything. Style is the most important word. I think we've lost some of the sense of what 'fashion' means. But I'll tell you why I don't think fashion is over. First, I don't think any of us know now what we're talking about when we say fashion. If you mean dictatorship of fashion, no one at the moment has anything to dictate. But once they do, we'll be very pleased and excited to hear it. Fashion is a rhythm controlled by the economic and social conditions of the times, and neither our social nor economic condition is very good. But I do think that clothes today are very pretty. There is a repose, a charm about the new clothes.

"I believe I just really like clothes. Peo-

ple want to be a little too deep about the whole thing. But I think all charming women will always have a sense of the refined, a sense of delight, and a sense of themselves. I don't envision a somber world. One likes certain things. For instance, I never thought the style of the thirties was remotely interesting, and I was living in a full world in those days. There

was no war, there was no visible depression in Europe, and Paris was absolutely remarkable. The clothes were beautifully composed and shown but they were never, to me, really interesting. I don't understand today's fascination with the clothes of the thirties. If you only knew how really weak they were after the clothes of the twenties.

"Today, I suppose Pucci and Gucci is good because it stimulates people toward a status symbol, but it keeps people apart. When I was in Beverly Hills I went down Wilshire Boulevard on a Saturday afternoon and saw crowds of cars and people. Usually there are never many people—after all, it's not a big city. And I said to my son, who was driving, 'Oh God, I hope it isn't an accident!' And he said, 'Good God no,

Diana Vreeland visits Kyoto with the Couture Show from the Met: Do it right, do it big, give it class! 55

that's just Saturday afternoon at Gucci's.' I just couldn't believe what I saw. All these men bring in girls that want to shop. That's all they want. At the end of the week it's 'Baby, I'll take you to Gucci if you're good.' This makes a lot of people happy, so put it down as good for business.

"You need a sense of humor in fashion, you have to see where you are. For instance, I've never tried wearing synthetics. It just never came my way. But I do remember one experience very well. I was motoring up to Maine for the weekend. I went to Brooks Brothers and bought myself a Dacron shirt, the copy of the men's pale blue button-down shirt—all the English and Europeans who came over bought them by the dozen and said they were marvelous.

"We got through Boston and it was terribly hot . . . we were in a traffic jam and we couldn't move. And you know, I thought I was in a fire! I had to open the shirt completely, I had to get out of it, and my husband said, 'In the name of God, what are you doing!' But I really and truly was in flames locked in this synthetic thing.

"I wouldn't have felt a chemical fire if I had been wearing pure cotton. It just would have been damned hot. But this was what I call an experience. Synthetics, however, have simplified the life of all of us. I suppose polyesters and so on are marvelous. They make clothes stand up and out and all that, which is great . . . for people who like it.

"It's been very curious, moving from a magazine to a museum, because now there are no daily deadlines. But the three shows I've worked on have been revelations. You think of the idea, and then of course, panic. Is it a good idea? Will it charm, pull and amuse the imagination? Can I pull it off? You don't know until you really work at it. But each show has been so marvelously revealing and wonderful. As you unpack the clothes coming from this museum and that, from Rome and Madrid, you look at them and you're so glad they're beautiful. It is never a letdown, never. It's always been just right! Now we have taken the couture show to the Modern Museum in Kyoto. It's the first time an Eastern museum has ever asked for a collection of European clothes.

"When I go through the Costume Institute at the Metropolitan Museum, one thing is more beautiful than the next, so well arranged, so well shown. Everything breathes, everything is free . . . they're alive, these clothes. You don't know how beautiful it is!

"Last year I used some Schiaparelli clothes from the thirties and we were very short of original hats. So we found some Southern Russian hats of the nineteenth century, all in solid silver embroidery, more or less the same shape, just like 'Schiap' used to make. I knew her collection well and these were absolutely suitable. It wasn't cheating in any way. You don't notice these things. You just see the effect and they're exactly correct.

"And for the Hollywood clothes exhibition, this dear gentleman asked, 'Would you be interested in Mary Pickford's curls?' He keeps them in a Baggie and I said, 'Where in the name of God did you get them?' He said, 'But she sent them to us for the Los Angeles Historical Museum.' Isn't that marvelous? After all, in all the world, those curls were the most special, just perfect . . . 'America's Sweetheart,' the first star, everything!

"In the beautiful gown from **The Bride Wore Red,** *Elizabeth Lawrence, who works on all the costumes, noticed that the bugle beads are all shaded as it fits the body. It's fantastic—the highest, highest couture refinement. It's total. I told a French couturier, 'You'll never find better-made clothes than these Hollywood outfits in any Paris workroom in the last forty years,' which is as far back as I can go. The great thing that went out across the studios from Louis B. Mayer when a new movie was being made in Hollywood was, 'Do it right. Do it big. Give it class!'*

"Those Hollywood designers knew how to dream up extraordinary clothes and dress beautiful women. You can always find great artisans. You can always get quality if you demand it.

"And what happens in five or ten years? Who's worrying? Every year I'm told it's the last Ball in Venice. All my life, the last Ball. But I've had a long life and gone to a hell of a lot of Balls. And life goes on very much the same."

YVES St. LAURENT

Sticking with the Classics

Yves St. Laurent is the top designer of our age. He is French, or rather Parisian: an elegant, understated perfectionist who makes it all look very easy, lazy, languid—and very sensual. His clothes for men and women are very special, very contemporary, but they always remain in style.

At thirty-eight, St. Laurent is still youthful. He has a strangely confident shyness, as if his slight smile is about to be captured by a flashbulb. After becoming the star designer of the House of Dior at twenty-one, he was drafted into the French Army, suffered a nervous breakdown, and came back to start his own couture house. St. Laurent is now part of a giant conglomerate, Lanvin-Charles of the Ritz, which backs his couture, jewelry, fabric, Rive Gauche ready-to-wear, accessories, perfume, and men's wear ventures. As an American retailer says, "St. Laurent is like money in the bank."

He speaks English slowly and shyly.

"It is good for me to come here, to New York. It is very exciting. The United States is going through the crisis we had in France after May 1968, like the consequence of the riots. Perhaps because they're not accustomed to this kind of crisis, this kind of depression, Americans are much more upset than in Paris, saying that life must change, that new things must come. On the street, I see only blue jeans. . . . This is the first time I have been in the United States when there is so little involvement in the fashion sphere. Perhaps it is because blue jeans give more confidence.

"This crisis, this depression, of course influences me in some way. More and more I believe in well-made, basic clothes with no 'fashion' that last many years without transformation—exactly like a blue jean. 'Classic' seems to be an old-fashioned word, but I think the contrary. A blue jean is a classic and I don't think it's old. I believe in basics,

LULU JOYEUSE

LULU TRISTE

LULU LUXE

QU'ON BRÛLE TOUT DO RÉ QU'ON BRÛLE TOUT DO MI SOL FA

LULU NÉRONE

LULU BATMAN

LULU DE BAR

LULU JUST A WOMAN

vilaine LULU MIDI-MINUIT

a wardrobe for a woman that is like a man's —exactly like a blue jean—pants, jacket, raincoat, not similar in details, but in mind. But if an amusing thing happens in fashion, why not try . . . but I don't like too much 'fashion.' Things must have a direction, a continuity.

"Now people are aware of their individuality more and more. To have style you must believe in yourself.

"The men's designs for St. Laurent Rive Gauche are exactly the same here as in France. I don't believe in special things for one country or another. Fashion is the same more and more. And more and more I don't think about the age of the woman or the man. There is no age to wear my clothes. They are basic. It is important to be yourself, not to want to look younger.

"Clothes are things that must last a lot of years without transformation. I like pure fabrics—cotton, silk, wool. I am unable to work with synthetics. Mixtures, yes, but synthetics have a contrary reaction for the body. I don't even like working with mixes, but what can we do? The time is coming in the world when a silk shirt will be a treasure.

"I find that prices are really too high. It's a question of the materials being so expensive. Everything is made in France. There are no workmanship problems, but to reduce prices I think the only thing to do is to be more and more specialized in a kind of clothes. Again, classics.

"The Paris woman in the past one or two years has been very exciting in fashion. Perhaps it was not so before. Recently Paris has taken a new vitality, new shape. There is a new woman with more sense of quality and refinement in life. A mixture of serious and giggle, a good balance in life for me. But the American woman has been the first image of the modern woman. It is a good experience to come here. In Paris perhaps, not to be pejorative, but because of all the continental traditions, they dress more seriously. France is full of traditions.

"A woman can feel very sexy in a chemise, as she can feel very sexy in jeans. It depends on the person. If she thinks she isn't sexy, she will not be sexy."

St. Laurent's cartoons of his mischievous little French character called Lulu.

SECOND-STRING CLASSICS

IVY LEAGUE AND WESTERN

Now that we've taken you through the never-never land of high finance and international tailoring, we want to tell you that it's all right: You don't have to spend all that money. If you want to look rumpled and tweedy without all the formality and expense of custom-made clothes and silk shirts, you can turn to the Ivy League look. Or if you want to look like the quintessential American, you can turn to Western classics.

THE IVY LEAGUE LOOK

Brooks Brothers has been called the Chanel of men's wear for sticking with the simplest designs year after year until they have become as classic and recognizable as a Chanel suit. The Brooks style provides a gently wrinkled old-money look in a range of subtle colors. These are the clothes you see on those mythic couples walking the deserted beach of Martha's Vineyard in early

The classic Brooks Brothers Ivy League casuals—stripes, Bermuda shorts and white bucks.

Parisian Ivy Leaguer in a reversible poplin raincoat.

spring, sipping a summer drink in Southampton, sitting on the terrace of the Ivy Club after a Princeton game, or browsing for antiques at a Chicago auction gallery. It is a very precise way of dressing, almost like an unwritten code, and one item of clothing seems to require the corresponding item. So although you can mix a Brooks look with jeans, dressing it down, you would drive classicists crazy by wearing Brooks

slacks with a shiny red ciré motorcycle jacket. But that's just what you should do if you feel like it.

The Ivy League look for summer runs something like this.

Shirt: An English cotton lisle polo shirt by Solly for the guy, a simple French cotton T-shirt for the girl. A pale blue, pink, or yellow button-down shirt under a light cable-knit sweater for both on cooler evenings.

Wear the shirt or T-shirt with yellow, tomato, or beige chino straight-legged pants, midwale corduroy slacks (perhaps in a bright color), corduroy jeans, or blue jeans. Belt the pants with solid-color webbing finished with leather closings.

On the feet: Weejun loafers or Top-Siders worn without socks.

When it gets chillier, the Ivy League dresser pulls a Shetland sweater or off-white Irish fisherman's knit over the shirt, with cords or jeans. The guy tops this off with an old tweed sport jacket that is meant to look as if it was handed down from his father (but could just as well have come from the local thrift shop). The girl pulls on an old tweed riding jacket or single-breasted blazer. In blustery weather, the old worn

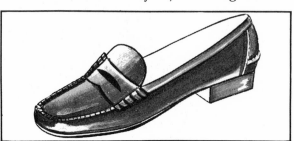

Brooks Brothers supplies the Shetland sweater and cotton shirt; Lauren Hutton supplies the sneakers and smile.

beige gabardine raincoat with reversible wool hounds-tooth check makes its appearance. These seasonal fashion changes are as dependable as the coming of autumn.

A modification of the Brooks look can be really stunning on a pretty girl. For instance, you could collect a few Brooks V-neck cashmere and wool sweaters in pale pastels and wear them big and baggy over tight Lee jeans and a pair of high-heeled, gray St. Laurent boots. Add some plain gold chains here and there and you have a look both boyish and sophisticated.

The rules of dressing in Ivy League classics can be almost as stiff and demanding as those of the custom-made universe. But this just gives you all the more room for innovation and invention within the basic form. Rules are made to be broken.

COWBOY CLASSICS

Cowboy clothes were once designed for survival on the range, but now they're our most popular home-grown classic. "Western clothes were originally survival clothes," wrote Jon Carroll in *Rags* magazine, "and

The essence of rodeo tailoring: country sequins.

First class examples
of "rodeo tailoring," both by
Nudie of Hollywood. Right:
Francois de Menil wears
a conservative maroon
and beige wool garbardine shirt
tailored to fit the body.
Above: a peach of a suit from
one of Nudie's old catalogues.
Add a buckskin skirt . . .
that's cowgirl heaven.

these elementary jeans, according to *Rags*, "tucked into the tops of heavy leather boots. A red flannel shirt was worn outside the trousers and gathered round the waist with a scarf of Chinese silk or a leather belt, or both, with a holster for a heavy Colt revolver. And any sort of hat . . . except the stovepipe beaver. They didn't want any class symbols out on the Great Frontier."

The custom-made leather jeans of today may not be class symbols, but they sure look classy. Those of us who bought them five years ago in the "latest" bell-bottomed style made a big mistake. The leather is still in great shape, but that hip-slung flared-leg fashion just doesn't look right today. The safest way to order leather jeans is as an exact copy of whatever jeans you've been wearing since you first played cowboys and Indians. The best leather jeans (often costing over $100) are so sturdy they can be pummeled, scrubbed, and stomped in the bathtub. You save on those exorbitant cleaning bills.

Another staple in the Western repertoire is the cowboy shirt. It's cut tight to the body (so it doesn't flap while you're riding),

their increasing relevance to our lives, along with the increasing relevance of the social and moral systems they symbolize, may say something about how close to the edge of the cliff of civilization we are."

Levi-Strauss jeans, as we've mentioned, are all-time classics. They began during the Gold Rush as sturdy trousers made of sailcloth, riveted with copper. The Americans and Europeans who headed west wore

Below: Cowboy Boots come in a dizzying array of colors, leathers and stitchings. What makes them a great investment is their rugged nature and timeless style.

yoked across the back and front, snapped on the sleeves and down the front, and flapped and snapped on the breast pockets. These shirts are especially handsome in plaids, ginghams, and solid colors, and take a bow tie or neck scarf with panache.

If you want conservative cowboy clothes, you can have them tailor-made by a "rodeo" tailor. We have seen beautiful wool gabardine shirts with contrasting yokes and white pearl snaps. One "formal" tailor-made jacket owned by a friend of ours has thirteen—count 'em, thirteen—buttons marching up the sleeve of the jacket, a sand and maroon gabardine trimmed with white piping on the yoke, patch pockets, and sleeves. It never fails to get a few conversations going during a stroll down Broadway. A really elegant way to wear these understated cowboy clothes is to put them together with jeans and a silk shirt for a party. It shows you care enough to make an extra effort to "dress," while letting you keep your own particular style of dress-up.

If you want even flashier cowboy clothes, send to Los Angeles for the catalog from Nudie the Rodeo Tailor. He does the rancher look as well as the gaudiest "parade class" around—electric colors, metallic trims, flashing fringe, sequins, and glittering jewels. If the Flying Burrito Brothers are your kind of rock group, Nudie's is your kind of store.

Cowboy boots are a well-heeled alternative to a pair of European "investment" boots. Although custom-made boots can easily run you up to $250, you can still find mail-order cowboy boots for under $100, custom-made to a drawing of your foot. The

prices are so reasonable because many Texas bootmakers use artisans over the border in Mexico. The design of the boot makes it good looking and sensible for the rider. The boot is shaped to give leverage in the saddle, the pointed toes get the arch into the stirrup fast, and the high heels catch the foot so you can't be dragged by the ankle. Genghis Khan and his Mongol warriors wore boots heeled with bright red to celebrate their fierce occupation and high status, but we can merrily outdo him. Joe Hall in El Paso

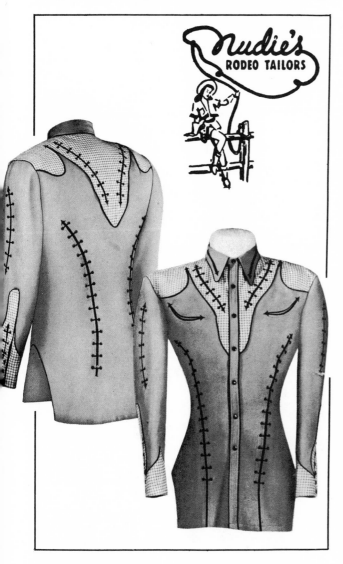

Today, just as in **1886**, feathers and leathers have a classy look. Left: A timeless style, that fitted custom cut of a classic Western shirt.

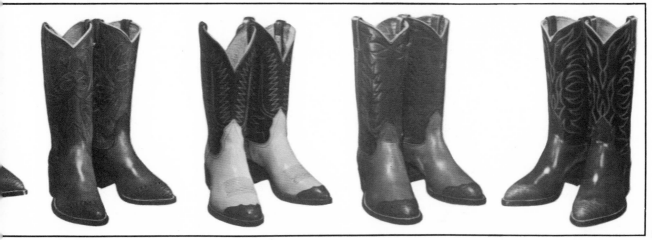

makes up boots in cowhide, veal, steerhide, calfskin, horsehide, kangaroo, boarhide, sharkskin, ostrich, elephant, and snakeskin, with bright colors to match. Some of his best customers are professional wrestlers, men who really know how to put on a show; the boots he creates for them are real show-boats.

Some Western boot connoisseurs think the most satisfying thing about their elaborately stitched and overlaid high-top boots is the fact that all that icing is never seen, except in the owner's closet. It's not exactly conspicuous consumption. But we think you should show them off. You can tuck jeans or jumpsuits into the tops of stovepipes. You can make a long skirt look different by wearing it with mid-calf boots, or alter the proportion of a big knee-length skirt with short boots. It takes a while to adjust to the look of it, but short or mid-calf boots look really new without being in the least bit nostalgic.

JEAN-PAUL GOUDE

Fashioning the Body Beautiful

Jean-Paul Goude is an art director of Es-quire magazine. His illustrations have appeared in major American and European magazines. He grew up in Paris with a French father and an American mother, and now lives in New York dreaming up ways to lengthen everyone's image, if not body. A meticulous artist, he combines photography and painting in such a personal and precise manner that you often cannot tell if you are seeing a picture or an illustration. Jean-Paul carries his personal brand of estheticism into his daily life and personal movie making.

"I've always art-directed my appearance. Naked, I have short legs. When I was a kid, I was doing men's fashion illustrations for Le Printemps department store in Paris. I gradually realized that these drawings were actually a projection of how I wanted to look. On paper I was elegant, long legged, broad shouldered, slim, etc. One day I decided to make the fantasy real, so I visited John Lobb, the bootmaker in Paris. Being conservative, I wanted a traditional shoe with no high heel, so the only solution was to have lifts put in them. I was twenty then. I still go to Lobb's. Now I'm six feet tall!

"Lobb shoes can cost up to $600, even more. It's not expensive because you get to wear them for ten years at least. I like white bucks too, and sneakers, but only with lifts.

"The American men's wear look is summed up for me by Brooks Brothers. It's not what it used to be, but it's still good when not trying to be 'continental.'

"I used to wear 'high-water' pants; you know, tight pants too short so you can see your socks (like Lil' Abner) because I liked the look of the rhythm-and-blues singers who used to perform in the Olympia in Paris. (That was in 1965, long before I came to live in the United States.) They were country boys and had a special style about them. I guess they were just 'country,' but to me they had a great look. I tried to wear 'high-waters,' but one has to be built like those guys to make it work.

"If one is small, one is almost forced to wear tight-fitting clothes. (James Cagney used to; so did Adolphe Menjou, even Fred

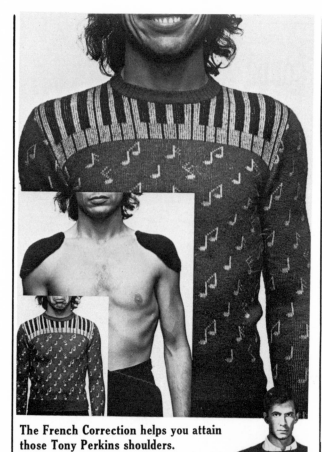

The French Correction helps you attain those Tony Perkins shoulders.
Add pads, glue them well and think tall. (No giggling!)

The sizzling energetic style of New York Puerto Ricans.

tions in their lapel. They were a reduced version of the tall English dandies, only they had brown Indian faces and shiny black straight hair. They really looked great. Porfirio Rubirosa had that look, except he was tall.

Good, better, best: noses in Jean-Paul's pantheon are OK on actor Jean Paul Belmondo, but the boxer at right has the truly perfect nose.

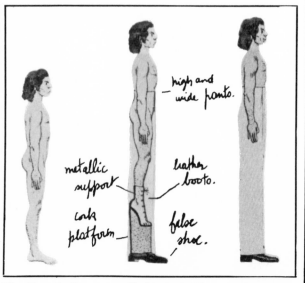

The French Correction II: To look like a fashion illustration, lengthen your lines with Jean-Paul's fantasy shoes. The normal shoe is buttressed with a towering cork platform, a metal support and lace-up boots and voilà, the designer's dream. (No wobbling.)

Astaire.) Did you ever see South American diplomats in the fifties, the ones who used to have their clothes made in Saville Row in London? They used to wear real tight jackets, rather wide trousers, and all the accessories; stiff collars, club ties, carna-

"In France, we have a certain idea of what Americans wear, and a lot of Frenchmen dress American when in fact Americans have stopped wearing these particular clothes, and are in turn wearing 'continental' clothes. Americans used to look great to us when they wore the Ivy League style. Now they wear Cardin suits which look like they are made of cardboard. It's a shame in a way, though I've seen some little French guys in their version of Brooks, and that can be sad too.

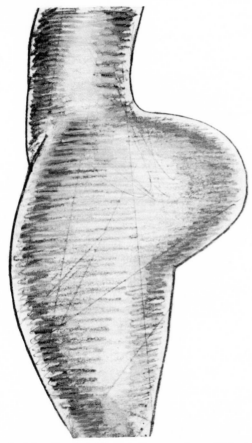

His ideal derrière is high, round, womanly and black.

"My tailor is Maurice Breslave. He used to be Eric Von Stroheim's tailor. Remember how great old Eric looked? Breslave still works for some of the best-dressed stars. He's the one who did those suits in the French movie *Borsalino*.

"Men are vain, but for some reason most of them think it's wrong to admit it. I guess they think it's not masculine.

"Tony Perkins used to look great in the late fifties before he started making films in Europe and tried to look French. He completely lost his style. He should go back to Brooks Brothers.

Sweatpants and white bucks with an impeccably tailored jacket, closed with an eccentric button at the neck.

The femme French Correction, or, Height is Pain.

"Don Robbie, St. Laurent's American men's wear designer, tried to capitalize on the way Puerto Rican teen-agers dress. He made them look like gangsters. I prefer to see those kids in their fifties thrift-shop clothes. They have such great taste and invention. It's funny, though, that it's the teen-age Puerto Ricans who have the taste. Through their influence Puerto Ricans have become the new ethnic stars.

"This reminds me of the 'Minets de L'-Étoile' when I was in my late teens. We were a whole gang hanging around the 'Drugstore' de L'Étoile in Paris. We wore blazers and flannel pants, trying to be very British. We came from the suburbs, not the elegant districts of Paris, but we looked more stylish than the rich kids. We were outdoing them with silk ties from polo clubs, monogramed shirts, cashmere scarves, and so on . . . I had a blazer made when I was about sixteen, and on the pocket was a gold embroidered emblem which I had copied from the golden eagle stamped on an American passport.

"My friends and I wanted to look like British clubmen and French race-horse owners. Consequently, I bought my first Rolls Royce when I was twenty-three, to complete the image; what I was doing actually was a softer European version of what black pimps are doing here. I never paid too much attention to physical characteristics at that time. I mean my face. But now, it's a different story. I always had a childish face because of my turned-up nose. The problem is, when you get a certain age and still have a kid's face you can easily look like an old

faggot. It's charming to have a kid's face when you're twenty-five, but I've just turned thirty-three, and I don't look so cute anymore. When I reach forty, I must have the 'face of a man,' a virile face. So I need a serious nose, not a kid's nose. If I had the nerve, I'd get a nose job. I'd have a boxer's nose done. But I don't trust plastic surgeons for myself because I'm too specific. I'd be scared they'd give me one of those obvious nose jobs. Too bad, I wouldn't mind looking like an ex-fighter when I'm forty.

"Mind you, I think plastic surgery and health spas will get so big they will be a threat to the garment industry. The better looking you are, the less clothes you need. In 1972, I started in Esquire the 'French correction,' in which I showed readers how to improve their appearance by wearing special shoes, shoulder pads in T-shirts, instant capped teeth, and so on.

"I still think it's a good idea, because people need advice before going into the hands of plastic surgeons who fancy themselves as modern versions of Leonardo Da Vinci, only they use a scalpel instead of a brush. I have seen so many rotten nose jobs done, I guess, by surgeons who could not draw. To become a truly great plastic surgeon, one should first win the 'Prix De Rome' in sculpture, then go into the medical profession.

"Sports are great to watch, not for the sport itself but for the way athletes move. I don't care much for ballet, but I've always liked dance and movement; that's why I'm a fan of Muhammad Ali. He's my favorite dancer. I think that most black fighters care more about looking good in the ring than actually winning a fight. Black people always dance whatever they do. I'm not a bleeding-heart liberal or a slummer. I like the esthetic of black people. Also, I think they are the most vital energy in American culture.

"Nowadays, my paintings as an illustrator tell anecdotes. I try to translate various assignments in the most sophisticated manner possible. But my stuff is sometimes too subtle, that obsession with style and good taste may hurt my career someday. For the time being, call me the 'Ernst Lubitsch' of illustration, and I'll be happy."

INGEBORG DAY

The Office Uniform with a System

Ingeborg Day is a thirty-four-year-old office worker in midtown Manhattan, mother of a twelve-year-old girl. She has devised a money-saving program called "Cost Per Wear" which she tells about here.

"In the winter I wear black. Two pairs of black pants, a black shirt, a black wool turtleneck, a fisherman's sweater, and a short-sleeved black sweater. I have a pair of black evening sandals and Italian boots.

"With all this black, the thing that I buy most often is tights. I never do comparison shopping for them, I just use the store that's closest to the office. I'm not going to stop wearing them if the price goes up, just like I'm not going to stop buying milk at the corner store. I get tights in special colors because it's the only color that shows in my clothes.

"In the summer I wear a pair of loose cotton pants in a purplish beige and a similar pair in blue, both two years old. This summer I bought some black drawstring pants. And last summer I went on a binge and bought three identical pairs of lined white slacks, two white t-shirts, and two white halters. They're all washable. In the summer I don't buy things that have to be

Plain pants subtly compliment an elegant dressing gown.

dry-cleaned. If you wear white and have three of each thing you can manage, even riding the subway and bus every day. I bought a white hat and a white skirt, and I wear white espadrilles. White is more practical than yellow, brown or even black, because you can use nurse's white shoe polish on the canvas—with any other color, there's nothing you can do if you spill something on them or someone steps on your foot.

"Summer and winter I wear a St. Laurent crepe de Chine skirt with narrow stitched-down pleats. I've had it since 1972, so I've worn it almost four years. It was on sale for $60, but the "Cost Per Wear" is small.

$$\frac{Price}{Number\ of\ times\ worn} = C.P.W.$$

$$\frac{\$60.00}{400} = 15¢\ per\ wearing$$

I've worn it at least 100 times a year over four years, so the CPW comes to 15¢ a wearing. In contrast, take what sounds like a cheap evening dress I bought on sale for $16 some years ago—I only wore it twice, so the CPW was $8. Compared with the 15¢ for my expensive skirt, that evening dress turned out to be a waste of money. Of course, people complain about my wearing black all the time—they say 'Has this become attached to your body?' or 'Didn't you sleep at home last night?'

"I don't dress up. No . . . that's not true, I do have three dress-up items: a Thea Porter dress, a Man Ray lip print a friend bought for me on sale for $30 that I've had since 1970, and a long black wool dress with a plain neck and no back which I bought because the designer and I both have the same first name. Recently my best friend gave me a long red velour wrap robe/dress from Betsey Johnson's.

"I always wear a simple ring given to me by my daughter, my mother's wedding ring, and a gold necklace with a guardian angel charm from my grandmother. It's all sentimental. In the summer I alternate two strands of pearls with the white T-shirts. I wear them so you can see them on the side and tuck them under the front. And recently a close friend gave me a scarab. 'It's like a pedigreed dog,' she said. 'It comes with a piece of paper, certifying that it's 3,500 years old, from such and such a dynasty.' It's now my favorite piece of jewelry.

"There are really only six areas of life you have to dress for. I've managed to get it down to three. The six areas are: bed, work, play casual, play elegant, sports, and social obligations. I've combined social obligations with play elegant. Sports, work and play casual have become the second category. Bed remains the third. If you also consider the time of year you can wear things, the clothes that fall into more than one season will give you the best CPW.

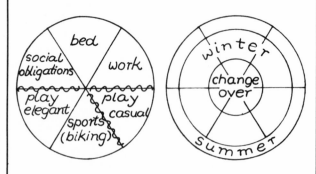

"On the east coast, winter would be the largest circle, but in other places, summer might be bigger. The French butcher's smock I just bought is going to have a low CPW because I can wear it in the summer with pants and espadrilles and in the winter with a turtleneck and boots, and all the times in between. I love it."

Uniform chic—the black T-shirt and pants with classic pearls and a Guatemalan bag.

FRAN LIEBOWITZ

Grouchy Simplicity

Fran Liebowitz is a magazine and script-writer of great wit and imagination, but when it comes to her own clothes she follows a strict line of quality and austerity. She owns very few clothes, yet always appears in well-tailored, neat outfits. Fran insists on following her basic ideas in getting dressed, for fear of wasting her energy on frivolity.

"I have no colors in my clothes. The most colorful I get is with two pale-pink shirts. I get too hot if there is red around me. I'm so particular about what I wear that my parents have been afraid to buy me clothes since I was six years old. I'm so conservative I still wear clothes from high school, but I haven't worn a dress in five years. It comes down to the idea that I don't like my clothes to make me stand out. To me, if anyone gets remarked on because of what they wear, they are badly dressed.

"I can't believe what some people wear. A great majority of kids in their late teens are the worst dressed . . . incredible platform shoes, glitter, hideous fabrics . . . useless extravagance.

"The only thing I ever regretted buying was this pair of black patent-leather shoes for $65 at Charles Jourdan. They're ridiculous, but I'll wear them until they fall apart. My most precious possession is a terrific riding jacket that was made a century ago for the aunt of a friend. She was eighty when she died, wearing it, and it is still holding up impeccably. The silk lining by itself is a beauty. I wear it with $2 white cotton sailor pants.

"A fan sent me a T-shirt inscribed with all sorts of ugly lines. I hate gimmicks and it prompted me to write a few paragraphs in Interview* magazine."

* ©Fran Liebowitz

Clothes with pictures and/or writing on them—yes, another complaint. Now I'm not just talking about Vuitton bags. Or Gucci wallets. Or Hermes scarves. Designers and/or business concerns who splash their names and initials all over overpriced accoutrements of dubious quality are of course exceedingly distasteful, but I am not talking about the larger issues. Open-necked deco-ish shirts with repeating patterns of middle-sized silhouettes of sailboats. Blue jeans depicting the death of Marilyn Monroe in waterproof pastels. Dresses upon which one (but preferably two) can play Monopoly. Overalls which remind toddlers, through the use of small pink animals spouting comic strip balloons, to brush their teeth. T-shirts which proclaim the illegal sexual preferences of the wearer. Ectetera. Ectetera.

"While clothes with pictures and/or writing on them are not entirely an invention of the modern age, they are an unpleasant indication of the general state of things, which encourages people to express themselves through their clothing . . . I mean, be realistic. If people don't want to listen to you, what makes you think they want to hear from your sweater?

"There are two main reasons why we wear clothes. First, to hide figure flaws, of which the average person has at least seventeen. And second, to look cute, which is at least cheering. If some people think that nice, muted, solid colors are a bit dull, they can add some punch with stripes, plaids, checks, or if it's summer and they're girls, small dots. For those of you who feel that this is too restrictive, answer me this: If God meant for people to walk around in coats that have pictures of butterscotch sundaes on them, then why does He wear tattersal shirts?"

ANTIQUES

SHOPPING THE THRIFT STORES

Up until a few years ago, wearing some stranger's old clothes was something only the poorest people did when forced to. Can you imagine your mother buying used clothes, except in an almost-new shop with prices to match? But as everyone is discovering, it feels good to wear expensive clothes, especially when someone else paid for them the first time out. And with the puffed-up prices of even moderate department store clothing, and today's shortage of natural fibers and good workmanship, it has become not only sensible but damned exciting to track down beautiful secondhand clothes.

Old clothes give you a sense of continuity with the past—an elegant way of life lived in luxurious fabrics of strict tailoring, a life of fluttering afternoon rituals and evening formalities. Solid old clothes give you a feeling that in this throwaway world

there are still some things around that can last ten, twenty, thirty, forty years, or more, and remain beautiful. And if you have the instincts of a bloodhound, they can be in your very own closet!

BEING CHOOSEY

There are a few things to keep in mind when shopping for old clothes. When you come upon something that appeals to you, ask yourself if the design is timeless. Will you be able to wear a thirties dress in a comfortable, contemporary style, or will it resist all your attempts to take away its strong costume look? Unless you prefer to wear costumes instead of clothes, you will not be happy with it. A costume takes a lot of energy to wear. It's usually going to wear you; perhaps wear you out (and that's not what you're after).

Secondly, is this discovery of yours in first-rate condition? Will the fabric hold up? Will the beading stay on? Will it come back in one piece from your friendly neighbor-hood dry cleaner? And has it been cleaned often enough in its past life? Or does some-one else's smell waft from the armpit of that glamorous but seldom-cleaned beauty? If it does, think twice. Perspiration may be chemically locked into the fabric, and each time you start to perspire in it, it will add its own unnerving scent—which won't be Chanel No. 5!

Third, if a piece of used clothing doesn't fit perfectly, is it close enough to your size to be fixed by a tailor or seamstress? Try it on. When thrift shopping, wear a leotard, tights, and a wraparound or button-front skirt. This way you can slip things on even if there's no dressing room. And if you like to wear high heels or boots, bring them along to get a sense of proportion when you try on dresses or pants. (Be careful with pants, because they often stretch to fit the ample aspects of just one person's derrière and can't be reshaped.)

Once you start collecting old clothes, line up a seamstress or tailor to help match up those brilliant discoveries of yours with the realities of your body. Because it seems that body shapes, as well as fashions, go in and

Jezebel is a top banana in New York's used clothing scene, specializing in droopy dresses and stiff Victoriana.

out of style every few years. (Witness Marilyn Monroe's Nike-missile breasts versus Twiggy's flat chest. Yet you want to wear both fifties and sixties things, right?) Make a pact with yourself to put aside the money to *make it fit*. Fit can make the least expensive find look very elegant.

You need a sensitive, able seamstress to make an old dress look as tasty as it did back in the forties.

TYPES OF SHOPS

There are several kinds of stores that sell used clothing. In a descending level of price (though not necessarily quality), there are the antique clothing boutiques carrying exquisite hand-finished antique dresses and couture clothes; the almost-new shops that hold clothes on consignment; private-enterprise boutiques, flea-market stalls, and thrift shops that pick over other thrift shop racks and sell you their finds for a markup. The privately owned youth-oriented thrift shops are where most of the action is, since they're a trendy compromise between department store and junk shop. They're popular because we don't all have the time and guts it takes to comb through hundreds of musty old thrift shops. These shops take the worry out of being cheap.

Los Angeles is a used-clothing haven. For some reason, perhaps the high glamour quotient of living near Hollywood and a tendency to treasure things that remind one of past dreams, southern California has the most accessible, appealing, best-quality clothes around. There are stores like Anne's-Tiques in Santa Monica that sell prim hand-starched and hand-ironed Victorian-era wedding dresses in absolutely pristine condition at a quarter of their price in New York. There are hundreds of thrift shops hidden amidst the waving palms, both charitable and not, classy and not-so-classy, as well as a thriving private business in selected secondhand clothes. With practice you can shop these stores as fast as your favorite boutique.

Lesley, a tough-minded English girl who always wears used clothes, shops nothing classier than thrift shops when she's working in Los Angeles. She has the time and the practiced eye to come up with some beguiling clothes, and she really can't afford to buy any other way. One of her most prized possessions is a perfectly preserved red satin jacket with bias-bound buttonholes and tailored cuffs by Don Loper, a grand designer-to-the-stars of the fifties era. She found this treasure for 95¢ at the downtown

Los Angeles Goodwill store. By always checking the labels in clothes she has become something of an expert on the shopping habits of fashionable Angelenos of twenty and thirty years ago. There is an I. Magnin label in her early fifties red wool coat. It hangs straight from the shoulder and is cut full in back with deep, cuffed sleeves. She found it for $2 at a thrift shop in Pasadena, a once-palmy area of Los Angeles now fallen on hard times. The fabric alone in the coat would cost $20 a yard today. Her favorite buy was discovered at

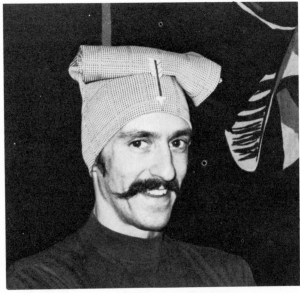

Waste not, want not: "Trouser leg snood" hides dirty hair.

Angeleno Antiques: Paul Ruscha's wardrobe comes exclusively from thrift shops and friends. The monkey fur coat was a trade-off with an actress; the Mylar eyeballs are the only new things he owns.

a Bekin's Moving and Storage sale that she saw announced in the paper. This knockout navy blue Marlene Dietrich-style blazer suit would have fit right in on a weekend with Marion Davies at Hearst's San Simeon. Inside the jacket pocket, where all custom-tailored labels are found, the former owner, date, and tailor are listed: Mrs. Tom May (of the family that owns the famous May Company department stores), 1936, Watson & Sons Tailors of Hollywood. The suit is totally lined with silk. To have it made

Cheap jacket, Victorian grouse foot and hunk of old fur.

today, at Bernard Weatherill Tailors in New York, would cost $400. It cost Lesley something like $3.

Lesley never fiddles with her clothes. "I never buy anything unless it fits. I like to keep the original length and proportion. I could never afford the quality I like in new clothes—that's why I buy old clothes. But I do spend a lot of time looking. It's the chase I love, the great discovery you feel when you're really struck by something!"

Artist/calligrapher Paul Ruscha is a neighbor of Lesley's who wears thrift-shop clothes as well as bits and pieces he trades around with friends or gets in exchange for his work. Artists who haunt thrift shops are always trying to one-up each other, and it leads to some very entertaining clothes! Paul's closet is hung on pipes, thrift-shop style, at one end of his studio. His prize is a monkey-fur coat given to him by an actress who got religion: she got a calligraphed Ten Commandments, and he got the coat. At night, Paul loves to go dancing in outfits like his white Tropicana Hotel pants with a blue silk, Isle of Capri, flare-collared, fifties shirt. Paul says you can always find Dior, Cardin, and St. Laurent shirts at the social aid societies ("like the Assistance League Thrift Shop on Fountain across from the Gas War"). Rich women have a quota of clothes they have to turn in to remain chummy with their friends at the league, so they bring in their hapless husband's almost-new shirts and go charge him newer ones. Paul figured all the young wives were doing this when he lived in Oklahoma City.

EXPERTISE

One of the reasons Susan Doukas moved to Los Angeles from New York was because of all the great thrift shops. Her taste leans toward unique, funny dresses with a lot of style, like her "Lauren Bacall" dress with gold studding on rust crepe and lots of sophisticated cutting. She's a definite believer in recycling, and says even when she gets rich she'll still go to thrift shops. "You can do really well if you have a little taste and not much money, especially if you look for beautiful things with a sense of humor. Certain clothes were really very silly, like the dresses of the thirties with all the intricate cutting and flaps and brooches. Dresses made statements of humor, and you could choose something you responded to because it was unique. Now fashion is just androgynous. Mass manufactured clothes have no individuality. Here are some of my pointers for shopping for used clothes:

1. Look for messy shops. A good one will have things like pants mixed up in the blouse bin. The very best bargains are in stores where you get really dirty, like the Volunteers of America in downtown L. A.

2. If you have a whole day and don't mind driving, hit the outlying areas, especially the old-guard suburbs, like Locust Valley out on Long Island.

3. Try to get an immediate sense of price. You can tell right off with shoes, first, then hats, picture frames, kitchenware. A glass for a nickel is cheap. Even though the stuff

Susan Doukas' favorite suit was once a size sixteen. It is now a size six, and she's made a bag from the leftovers.

may seem depressing one day, remember shops really vary because they constantly get new shipments.

4. You must wash things to kill the bugs, and that bothers some people! If there's a smell or stain, I just scrub and scrub and send it to the cleaners. But remember, for $8 you can get the most absolutely gorgeous thirties or forties crepe dress. And if you take it in, you can make a drawstring purse from the leftover fabric.

5. If salesladies want to help you and follow you around, avoid the shop. It's not worth it. I prefer a place where I can barter. Say I find a $1.50 sweater with a couple of buttons missing or a hole in it. Usually it's okay to say, 'Can I have it for a dollar?,' especially if it's a Christian organization. In the Jewish ones they don't usually let you bargain—they just say, 'No, honey, the price is marked.' "

When a group of friends all thrift shop, they can help each other develop collections. Susan, for instance, has a closet full of bowling-league shirts and soft-drink-delivery-man's uniforms.

| **Susan insists her style is silly rather than chic, but she always pulls off an individual look with special moxie.**

Valentina has to put together a wardrobe on the small salary she makes as production assistant and receptionist on the Cher Show. She tries her best in the midst of all that Bob Mackie-designed Cher glamour to pull off a special look. She likes to mix the old with the new, and for her the private-enterprise used-clothing store is the best bet. In the funky Silverlake section of Los Angeles where she lives is a typical shop called Aardvark's Odd Ark. Used clothing chosen with an eye for the younger customer is arranged on racks by category: used jeans, plaid shirts, overalls, Levi jackets, forties and fifties tailored jackets, suits, beaded thirties dresses, bias-cut nightgowns, Mexican felt jackets, and a multitude of sins. The most outstanding and high-priced items are displayed on the walls above the racks, rather dusty, but often the only decor in this type of low-overhead operation. And where do the clothes come from? Shops ranging from Aardvarks's on up to the used chic of Yesterday's News near Beverly Hills buy their goods from out-of-the-way thrift shops or from the sinister-sounding "rag houses" in downtown Los Angeles. Ropa Usada is one of these rag house warehouses. Room-sized bundles of clothing from the Midwest are piled to the ceiling and sold in one-thousand-pound lots without being cleaned. A thousand pounds of clothes can run $200 to $500. The bundles then have to be sorted by the buyer and the best things winnowed out and cleaned. Some of the smaller dealers complain that the used-clothing business is getting so profitable it's being run like the Mafia, that Beverly Hills-style boutiques have a complete monopoly on the rag house bundles.

People in the West and down South hold outdoor swap meets year-round, while others have to wait for the summer months. One of the Angelenos' favorite gathering spots is the Hollywood Swap Meet, located in an empty corner parking lot on Santa Monica Boulevard in West Hollywood. It's a lively area filled with picnic tables, makeshift dressing rooms, and jerrybuilt clothes racks. Just plain folks as well as Zsa Zsa Gabor, Ruth Buzzi, Lena Horne, Shelley Winters, Sonny Bono, Carol Lynley, and

Valentina eyes the reindeer rack at her local L.A. store.

Cher drop by to try stuff on. The sellers rent space to display their wares and the lot is open every day of the week. We found an apricot, hand-sewn crepe de Chine bed jacket for $2; beautiful pure silk nightgowns with hand-stitching and hand-made lace appliqués (perfect for transferring to a T-shirt or dress if the rest of the fabric is frayed) for $3 to $10; hundreds of pairs of used jeans arranged by size for $4 or $5; Air Force flight suits for $25–$35; sailor tops, military uniforms, and safari jackets, and typically Californian standbys like kimonos, Mexican felt jackets, Oriental-theme satin baseball jackets, and Hawaiian print shirts. (The best-priced and most amiable stall is run by Ruthie, but she's only there on Fridays.) Another popular swap meet is the massive gathering held on weekends in the Hollywood Bowl. It's so big it can make you dizzy.

San Francisco is a tremendous place to find stylish used clothing because of the flashy transvestite and gay scene crystallized by the Cockettes in the early seventies. Stores that cater to this taste, like Casey's Faded World and the Flying A, have higher prices but very select merchandise. It's nice to have a gay friend—he can often steer you in the direction of the most chic, and the most cheap, shop in your town.

It's always smart to get shopping advice from people who make money from their clothes. Carrie White, who runs a beauty salon in Beverly Hills, rented out some things from her personal wardrobe for the film *Shampoo*, set in 1968. ("1968, can you believe it! They're already being collected!")

Carrie says to stake out five thrift shops rather than spreading yourself thin over fifteen. Whenever you travel, check the most remote places for shops (like Cathedral City, which is ten minutes out of Palm Springs), or at least go one block off the main drag. She looks first for colors and patterns that will ease her eyes when she sees herself in the salon mirror at work. She always checks the thrift-shop drawers, which a lot of people forget, and finds doilies, ribbons, scarves, bathing suits; napkins which make great skirts and pieces for lengthening jeans; and white lace to lengthen white pants. And since Carrie has four kids, she's always looking for children's hand-crafted clothes. Carrie loves the sport and the fun of it. "In nine years, no customer has ever seen me in the same thing twice!"

Another person who makes money by

The ultimate luck is to dig up a twenties extravaganza in a musty, old thrift shop. When luck strikes, spend.

collecting old clothes is Steve Starr. The Steve Starr Studio in Chicago is home for a truly spectacular collection of period clothing, some for sale. Steve says he collects "art deco, art moderne, art ultra, and twentieth-century costumes and accessories." Every year he stages the Steve Starr Vanity, which stars his clothes, decade by decade, worn by an all-singing, all-dancing, cast of clothes freaks and models parading through a series of elaborate production numbers and film clips. It may well be the most entertaining event of the year in Chicago, a home-grown *That's Entertainment*. Since he has so many first-quality dresses and accessories, he is often reluctant to sell his favorites, which he keeps for the Vanity and

Ingrid Boulting discovered this funny fifties bit of Orientalia in an out-of-the-way Goodwill Store.

uses in producing and styling photographs, many for *Playboy*. He's now working on a full-color collection of these photos, which should be a tremendous source book for period clothes.

In London, the painter Duggie Fields and about twenty or thirty friends put on their own "jumble sales" by hiring a church hall and bringing things to sell. "The rental goes to the church charities, and what we make we keep for ourselves. We advertise the sale in the local papers, list it in *Time Out* magazine, and design posters to put in neighborhood shops. Hundreds of people come. It's fun, and it's a good way to get rid of your old stuff and get new from your friends. It's good recycling, and at the same time you can make $100 in an afternoon just for cleaning out your closet.

"The clothes are all piled up—our first jumble sale was chaos—and as soon as the doors open, people run in, grabbing. It's like being in a chicken coop. But it's a nice afternoon, and it's fun to see who turns up. I even see people stealing. They know I know they haven't paid, but I'm not going to say a thing . . . things gotta go!

"I only buy clothes in stores if I need something I can't find here. They're not necessarily fashionable stores. My favorite is called 'Sex' in the World's End . . . bits of furs, porno embroidered T-shirts, and humorous clothes. My idea of wearing clothes is to make myself smile. I like that in others too. I don't think clothes should be serious."

In New York, the used clothing prices

Duggie Fields' sensibility is born of jumble sale chaos.

are much higher than they are in Europe or on the Coast. Some of our favorite stores in New York are Everybody's Thrift Shop, Jezebel (on the West Side), Cherchez!, and Lune en Papier (in steeply ascending order of price). Henri Bendel is now carrying antique Victorian dresses at prices that range around $500. And that is a bit beyond the range of Cheap Chic, no matter how finely detailed and irreplaceable they may be!

One of the best places to find rich New Yorker's castoffs is where they vacation, like the Palm Beach Thrift Shop in Florida. Beautifully tailored three-piece suits can be found here for $10, and with tailoring, a suit for the office can cost only $35. One New York businessman has three $10 English-tailored suits he bought at the Palm Beach Thrift Shop: two formerly lived in New York, one in Chicago. Along with a navy cashmere coat from Sak's, also used, they make up his entire office wardrobe, and no one is any the wiser.

Blondes do have more fun, especially when they're hiding behind an old-fashioned mysterious bit of veiling.

The Duggie Look: His paintings are a pastiche of Miro, Arp and Dali; his clothes are an aggressive blend of forties, fifties and sixties, tied together with eccentric bits of embroidery and squiggles. And check those shoes.

ANTIQUES

For some fashionable women, the ultimate chic is dressing in couturier clothes of the past. An eccentric editor at Italian *Vogue* dresses entirely in antique Poiret couturier originals that are terribly elegant yet contemporary in feeling. Who could make a more glorious dress than Schiaparelli, or a more elegant suit than Chanel? If you set your sights on originals like these, you have to be extremely lucky (of course, the first step to "luck" is to learn as much as you can about the couture), and it helps to cultivate rich relatives or friends, unless you are prepared to spend your life's savings!

Most of the truly classic couture clothes are now being donated by estates to museum collections for the inevitable tax write-offs. Thousands of beautiful things are locked away in the climate-controlled storage rooms of the Chicago Historical Society, the Metropolitan Museum, and the Museum of the City of New York. Entire wardrobes, right down to the needle-toed, stiletto-heeled Charles Jourdan black faille pumps, arrive by chauffeured limousines and are carried into these grand museums, never to be worn again except by plaster mannequins. Some designer clothes are still at large, though they are increasingly rare. The owner of an antique clothing shop in New York has two St. Laurent couture dresses, because, she says, "they are a lot nicer than the things that are being made now. I bought them for a good price and can resell them at a reasonable profit. I've been collecting clothes for about ten years, going to places like Canada and south to Georgia, but now it's costing too much to go out and look." She has sold a Chanel, a St. Laurent, and a Fortuny dress. If you don't have hundreds in disposable income, your best bet is to try Canada and Georgia yourself!

GREAT FINDS

When shopping for used clothing, whether you are in a pricey on-consignment store or a dirty old thrift shop, be sure to keep your eyes peeled for the following:
Luscious fabrics, like pure **silk,** in nightgowns, slips, loose undershorts, chemises, bed jackets. All sorts of scarves, especially the $1 bias-cut, long, thirties silks (now selling at around $30 in antique clothing shops). Well-cut silk shirts. Lovely silk

Expert thrift-shoppers keep their eyes peeled for pure silks like this arty-looking, loose-cut blouson.

neckties, silk squares, and neck scarves.

Cotton petticoats, lace shirts, Victorian dresses with tight bodices, men's and women's shirts, straight nightgowns, cowboy shirts, cotton flannel plaid shirts, pedal-pushers, slacks, and safari outfits.

Pure **wool** is found in women's tailored suits, coats of gabardine, melton, cashmere, tweed, and challis, tight or big mid-calf skirts, and sweaters. If you're looking for a sweater, be sure to look through the children's bin, because the French size their sweaters 1, 2, and 3, and the ladies who work in volunteer thrift shops aren't going to know this, but you are. In fact, it helps to familiarize yourself with European sizing.

The French sizes 1–2–3– for T-shirts run a bit tighter than American S–M–L, because the French prefer shirts to be a bit more clinging. English dress sizes usually run one size smaller than American. A size 10, for instance, would be the equivalent of our 8. And continental sizing for dresses, blouses, pants, sweaters, and so on runs 38–40–42–44, roughly the equivalent of 6–8–10–12. For slips and bras, 80–85–90–95 is 32–34–36–38. European shoes don't have the range of widths ours do, and the sizes 36–37–38–39–40 are roughly 5 – 6 – 7 – 8 – 9. Of course, as with anything you find at a thrift shop, try it on.

Men can look for beautiful wool overcoats, tailored suits, sport jackets, formal evening wear, fifties Eisenhower jackets, letter jackets, and pleated slacks. A tailor can make you feel like a million bucks for an investment of $25 and a morning spent digging through likely looking shops. A

True costumes like this demand a self-confident stance and a bit of discipline, qualities exuded by the two sisters, above. Such old clothes were once cared for by a battery of seamstresses, laundresses, dressmakers and ladies' maids. Delicate antique clothes still demand very special hand care and a slower, self-contained manner of moving. Start dancing, and precious old fabrics rip and shred and seams reach the breaking point.

An original among originals, Bill Cunningham creates this apparition from bits of antique feathers and fluff.

slim woman can look beautiful in a man's suit if she has it tailored to fit perfectly and wears it with the humor of Bianca Jagger: walking stick, hat and veil, a crisp cotton shirt or a bright silk blouse unbuttoned practically to the waist, with a tiny gold chain underneath.

Another material to look for is beautifully worn **leather,** which can always be relined; tent-shaped trenchcoats for men or women, suede jackets and sport jackets, brown or black motorcycle jackets with a diagonal zipper. Some people have good luck with shoes, like worn brown English oxfords, expensive old high heels, and weatherbeaten riding boots.

And for extraspecial evenings: fur boas, pleated or gathered taffeta skirts, soft velvet dresses or smoking jackets, all sorts of fancy cocktail dresses and ball gowns, and men's velvet evening jackets. One friend of ours found custom-made tails with a label from Barcelona for $5, including the

Model Apollonia von Ravenstein with stylist Ara Gallant: She always wears the oldest, slinkiest dress on the block.

starched front. His tailor fit it to him for $30, and the couple of times he's worn it to formal parties he's had great fun imagining the stiff and rather large Spaniard who inhabited the tails before he did.

So, if you want to be cheap and stay ter-

ribly chic, remember that your best allies are thrift shops, used-clothing stores, antique clothing boutiques, swap meets in empty lots or out-of-town drive-ins, European flea markets (like Portobello Road in London, the Thieves Market in Amsterdam, or the Marche aux Puces in Paris), street fairs, block parties, and individual garage sales. If you're still unfulfilled, have your own "jumble sale."

A little-known bit of forties chic: The "captain's dinner jacket" in a light wool gabardine, from the collection of Chicago's Steve Starr Studio, worn by Mr. Starr himself.

If you have to go white tie, try the thrift shop route. A fifties spaghetti-strap gown is the perfect companion.

DISCOUNTS

Aside from all these used-clothing resources, smart dressers have always known that you can finish off a look very cheaply at mass-market discount and five-and-dime stores. Great bargains are there for the finding at chains like Woolworth's: smock tops;

Thrift shops are a godsend for parents on a tight budget. You can always find kids' wonderful hand-made things here.

An antique Philippine tea dress Larissa found at Harriet Love's in N.Y. Without an underslip, it's a party dress.

printed, pleated, or visored scarves; arm-loads of beads, pearls, and plastic bracelets; hooded sweatshirts and pants; bikinis or $1 Rio-style pants; short shorts; plain and souvenir T-shirts in cotton and terrycloth; country bandanas; summer shifts; and lots of interesting shoes, like the plastic, fisherman's Mary Jane, a ballet slipper flat you can wear on the street, the Japanese rubber-and-straw-soled shoe with a velvet thong, and the canvas cross-strapped old ladies' shoe. The drawback these days with the discount chains is that they are trying to merchandise "looks," which means that the quality of the fabric and construction is going down while you pay more for a "fashion" that will probably bore you next

Sofi Bollack and little Eleonore created the lush look of Victorian teatime with the help of a friendly thrift shop and plump pillows made of fancy remnants.

year or even next month. Too bad, but you can still snoop around and find classic designs if you persist.

Big-volume department stores, like Alexander's, Ohrbach's and Macy's, often carry the newest ready-to-wear looks from Europe at very low prices, but you have to shop carefully and know just what you're looking for so you don't get swamped by all the merchandise.

Ethnic shopping areas will often yield great buys. In New York, Jewish merchants sell their wares in crowded stalls on Orchard Street, and a lot of almost-wholesale buys from Seventh Avenue manufacturers are mixed in with the cheap merchandise. Also on the Lower East Side are the Russian shops around St. Mark's Place, which carry about the same merchandise as the government-run tourist shops in the capitals of Eastern European countries—peasant blouses, challis scarves, carved wood boxes, painted eggs. On Fourteenth Street there is a vast hubbub of Puerto Ricans shopping discount stores with bins

The formal social dance of the past has been bypassed by the hustle of today. But by outfitting ourselves in luxurious antique clothing, we can afford to partake in the old rituals. Here, Pierre Clementi in Steppenwolf approximates fin de siecle seriousness.

The jacket: Chinese silk brocade. Era: pre-Communist. Point of purchase: Palm Beach Thrift Shop, $10 (plus tax).

along the sidewalk, and way uptown is La Marqueta, the enclosed Puerto Rican market area with stalls running under the elevated tracks of the New York Central Railroad. These street markets are not limited to clothing and household goods—you can always pick up some compatible food, like blinis on St. Mark's or Caribbean plantains in La Marqueta.

Some people stroll by Fifth Avenue department store windows for entertainment, but shopping older urban areas can be a much less expensive pastime. No matter what city you visit, seek out the old neighborhoods with their thrift shops and discount stores. You can spend a fine afternoon looking for wonderful bargains, and finish it off by devouring an adventurous local meal.

Genevieve Waite loves her
soft apricot crepe de Chine bed
jacket for summer parties.
Totally hand-stitched,
it was $2 at the Hollywood Swap Meet.
Her son Tamerlaine is less fond
of his new school uniform.

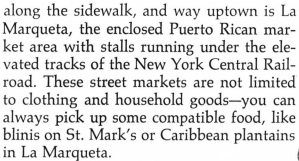

NANCY CROW

If It Feels Good, Wear It

Nancy grew up and went to college in Minnesota and moved to New York, where she works in a publishing house. Her philosophy of dressing is "if it feels good, wear it."

"I think you gotta keep your head straight about clothes—they're entertainment. After I went through the whole Peck & Peck conservative college girl thing in Minneapolis, I realized that fashion is actually wearing things that feel good together, that delight you, and knowing that 'bad taste' is just a figment of someone else's paranoia. I don't worry if I 'coordinate,' because somehow it always all falls into place. I don't ever take myself seriously; I enjoy. A friend of mine said I dressed like a circus, 'but for a clown, you certainly look gorgeous most of the time.'

"My clothes are fun. They're just a collection that's evolved over the last six years, one thing here and one thing there. And it all pleases me. That's what clothes are for, aside from protecting you from the rain and giant armadillos, you know.

"I don't shop. If the moment is right, I know it. If the thing, the money, and I are all together, that's my cue. But aside from things like sweatsocks or safety pins, I rarely go out to buy something. You may find something you like in a department store, but there are miles of racks, and you can see yourself on the street four times in one day. I prefer small, out-of-the-way places. The people are nicer, and such places are really not more expensive. Get to know a few good little places and stop in every now and then.

"There's no one thing in my closet that I love—everything is my favorite. I never get up and think, 'I don't have a thing to wear!' It's just a matter of what I feel like mixing. The basic secret of having a style is confidence—you exude it, and people assume that what you wear is not only fashionable, but way-the-hell-ahead-of-them chic. It's a savvy you have about your clothes, and with savvy you can get away with anything.

"I try to do a kind of 'lateral thinking' with old clothes. I took a hand-sewn, beautiful silk bed jacket, cut it in tight, added lacing across the bodice, and now it's a really sexy top for evening. I found an antique ivory velvet dress cut like a Vionnet—it had stains under the arms, but I fixed it by cutting them deeper; that made it much sexier, too. But it was one of several of my 'finds' my father threw down the incinerator—he was offended because I'm no longer 'Peck & Pecked.'

"Last year I probably spent about $150 on clothes. My boots are from 1970. I bought two pair of shoes in the past year for about $25 each, and a few this's and that's when lightning struck. I buy only things that I love and will love until they drop off me or the hanger. I have an acrylic knit skirt with an outrageous palm tree design that I found in some little shop in Minnesota in 1969; I just went straight to it. If you know what you like, you can make terrific finds in places like K-Mart, the Canal Street Flea Market in New York, and the Rag Factory in Minneapolis; even from your relatives and friends. I bought a winter maxicoat for $130 in 1969, and it's served me well each winter since. It's immensely warm, a lasting classic design.

"I do spend money on good jewelry—gold is warm, and platinum is class. If you live in it, you assume a certain haute, which is getting back to attitude.

"That is the basic, a sense of ease and a sense of humor. But always, the awareness of our time limit. We're only human; we deserve to enjoy."

The hat above is an authentic bowler from Dunn & Co. of Great Britain. At right, an antique piano shawl of apricot satin, lavishly embroidered and fringed is wrapped around a Biba T-shirt. A grey crepe 1930's dressing gown with a gathered Indian cotton print top, worn as a vest is combined with a Capezio hat and bias silk scarf.

EWA RUDLING

Ragpicker Deluxe

Ewa Rudling is a deluxe ragpicker. She directs and paints her life in muted tones. In her large white-and-silver Paris photography studio everything is mobile. Ewa uses all of her furniture and her own clothes as accessories in her detailed and refined photographs.

"I want to be like a mop of quality. Nobody can ever say I look dirty, because I dress on purpose in dirt tones. I dye most of my clothes dust brown, dust gray, and so on. A few years ago I saw the film Trash and was shocked to see someone furnishing their house with things retrieved from garbage and getting dressed out of rags. At that time I was really living in luxury with a wealthy husband in a three-floor house surrounded by a garden.

"When I left, it was total poverty and a long struggle. When you are, or when you become, poor, you also become very inventive. You find yourself taking in things you normally would not have looked at before. Like an ant, you gather other people's discards that, with a little thought, they could put to use themselves.

"After a while I accumulated so much stuff that I started making money from it to pay for my photography. I would hold 'chiffon parties'—I would take all the things I thought were good to sell: clothes, jewelry, objects, suitcases, shoes, hang them all over the studio, and let everyone know that a sale was going on. People would bring other people and I would get rid of all the clothes in one go, and often also acquire new ones or simply exchange. It's the best way to clean out your closet and make money.

"Of course, by that time you have left your pride far behind you . . ."

SPORTS

At one time, sportswomen looked precisely like sportsmen—there was no room for good looks in competition. But now we can have our cake and eat it too. Style is so free we can look as feminine in a man's football jersey as we can in a ruffled tennis dress. Today, more and more women are wearing professional athletic clothes as an almost day-in, day-out style of dressing. There are several reasons for the popularity of authentic sportswear, but their main attraction is functional, unchanging, unflappable design. Sports clothes are built for speed, endurance, power, and winning. And who can't use a little injection of that in everyday life?

With the advent of color TV, pro sports picked up electric acrylic colors—the Oakland A's suited up in Fort Knox gold, trimmed with Pacific Ocean green; and everyone acquired a taste for nice, tight-fitting, stretch uniforms over well-muscled, shapely bodies. Professional athletes say that looking good makes them play better; their uniforms give them that winning feeling.

Also, some sports clothes offer the cheap thrill of discovery. A Cheap Chic adept is going to go out and find the ones that haven't been discovered by Seventh Avenue because they offer economy with true style.

Last year a friend of ours was driving through Ireland and stopped at an out-of-the-way sporting-goods shop in Galway hoping to discover some new well-designed uniform. The soccer things looked rather promising—those great T-shirts and striped socks—until she got back to London and visited Biba's department store, where the soccer motif had been so thoroughly run through the fashion grinder that little 75¢ soccer-ball-shaped change purses were up for sale next to the cash register. She decided there was nothing left to discover on God's green earth. But then came the import of the sport of motocross, still relatively unknown outside southern California and the Northeast, where the major events take place. She discovered a whole new world of clothes—high, sturdy leather boots with bright contrasting panels in the front, and beautifully cut pants with diagonally quilted leather pads along the sides of the hip and thigh. She was ecstatic. Since she was tall and skinny, the motocross pants looked great, despite the padding.

The cheapest places to find authentic

105

American cheese of sportswear, bristling with unnecessary buttons, flaps, cuffs, and seams. Sports clothes still have the magic of childhood game clothes.

FLEET OF FOOT

Warm-up suits give you that fast-on-your-feet look even if you don't jog or play tennis every day. What thief would risk snatching your purse if you look like a champion sprinter? **Warm-up suits** are being manufactured in more styles and brighter colors. If you feel conservative, buy yourself a high-school-style warm-up suit in gray, fuzzy-lined sweatshirt material with a front-pocketed top. It's as comfortable for sleeping on cold nights as for shopping on crisp afternoons. The gray sweatshirts can also be dyed in darker colors to fit your mood. A $7 sweatshirt can be ordered from J. C. Penney's catalog in pale blue, yellow, red, or green, with matching $7 snug-fitting sweatpants, which won't look or feel as floppy as the loose, baggy, sixties style. Oleg Cassini makes a jersey warm-up and competition set with jacket, pants, sleeveless T-shirt, and tiny shorts, all in bright colors. The women athletes wore them for the ABC-TV Women's Superstar event at the Astrodome. Suzy Chaffee looked especially snazzy in her acid-yellow short-shorts combined with multicolored Peruvian-style patterned knee socks and black professional warm-up shoes.

Tennis whites are so popular these days that demand is rumored to be more than

athletic clothes are sometimes out of the way, but it's worth bypassing your expensive local pro shop or tennis boutique. The best way to buy professional athletic wear is to look up sporting-goods stores in the Yellow Pages and give them a call. If they don't have what you're looking for, it's almost as convenient to order things by mail. You'll have to ask a male friend for a size approximation if you're sending for boys' or men's sporting uniforms, but if they don't fit, most mail-order houses will usually exchange them. Try the big mail-order catalogs, and for the less-popular uniforms, like rugby or soccer, send for information from the manufacturers listed in the back of this book.

The good feeling you get from honest-to-goodness sports clothes comes from their purity of design. They haven't been through the fashion mill of Seventh Avenue, and they still have that legitimate feeling. They're not yet made into the processed

the manufacturers can churn out. In the suburbs, many women have taken to wearing inexpensive, easy-care tennis dresses as their everyday uniform. If you have nice legs, a tennis dress gives you a good excuse to show them off. One problem with tennis dresses these days is that they have become a fashion item, and dashing, simple design has given way to all sorts of "cute" motifs and silly details. Tennis stars like Billie Jean King and Françoise Durr wear these flashy dresses because they consider themselves, quite rightly, to be in show business. Are you?

Sneakers are basic Cheap Chic footwear. It used to be that fashion started at the top and worked its way down; the feet were just an afterthought. But here we are in an era of tight money, and we don't have that much to spend on body coverings. To save money, we can displace our fascination with the minutiae of style and status to the foot—a foot dressed in a very expensive permutation of what was once a cheap shoe, the sneaker. Sneaker demand is up almost 25 percent this year. Of course, the sneaker is not only stylish, it's Good for You, like chicken soup on a cold day. Sneakers bring you back to childhood, high spirits, and magically high leaps.

In the haute monde of sneakerdom there is a competition of status symbols which easily rivals the Fifth Avenue battles of Gucci, Hermès, and Mark Cross. Sneakers don't have designers' names, they have signs: stripes, wedges, chevrons, and stars of status. And they have endorsements by the new media stars, athletes like Billie Jean King and Walt "Clyde" Frazier.

It started with the war between Adidas and Puma, companies owned by feuding German brothers. *Sports Illustrated* did an exposé on their buy-out of the athletes at the Mexico City Olympics, and for the first time, Cheap Chic students were exposed to the full stylistic possibilities of $30 leather-and-suede athletic shoes. Wrestling shoes, boxing shoes, high-tops, training shoes, track shoes, football shoes, soccer shoes, officiating shoes, tennis shoes, handball shoes! It was a mere hop, skip, and a jump from track and basketball shoes into tennis shoes and out onto the streets. Now you can choose from the Converse star, Pony chevron, Adidas triple stripe, and the Puma flying wedge. Somehow, those $11.98 Levi's feel a lot livelier when a pair of $30 wear-forever leather sneakers is peeking out under the cuff! If you want a man's sneaker, buy them 1½ sizes smaller than women's sizes.

SPEEDSTERS

Grand Prix drivers have highly romantic images. Just think of Paul Newman, Jackie Stewart, Steve McQueen, or Mike Hailwood. Yet the actual competition uniforms for speed are terribly uncomfortable and

The precision of a chronometer when seconds count.

hot. Their function is to protect the racer from contact with the ground at speeds hovering around one hundred miles per hour; and, in the case of Formula cars, to protect the driver from fire in case of an accident. None of these uniforms really breathe, which is one reason, along with fear and excitement, why professional racers often sweat off six pounds driving a two-hour race. But if you want to look like a Grand Prix driver without all the sweat, you can find Nomex-style, one-piece, mechanics' jumpsuits like the drivers wear. Bright orange is the sexiest color. Tight is the sexiest fit. (You'll need a seamstress to get it tight, unless you're a sewing-machine genius.)

Motorcycle gear, no matter how hot or uncomfortable, is still an evocative style of dress. "Leathers" have symbolized anger,

Racy jumpsuits built with style for speed and adventure.   109

Antonio 74

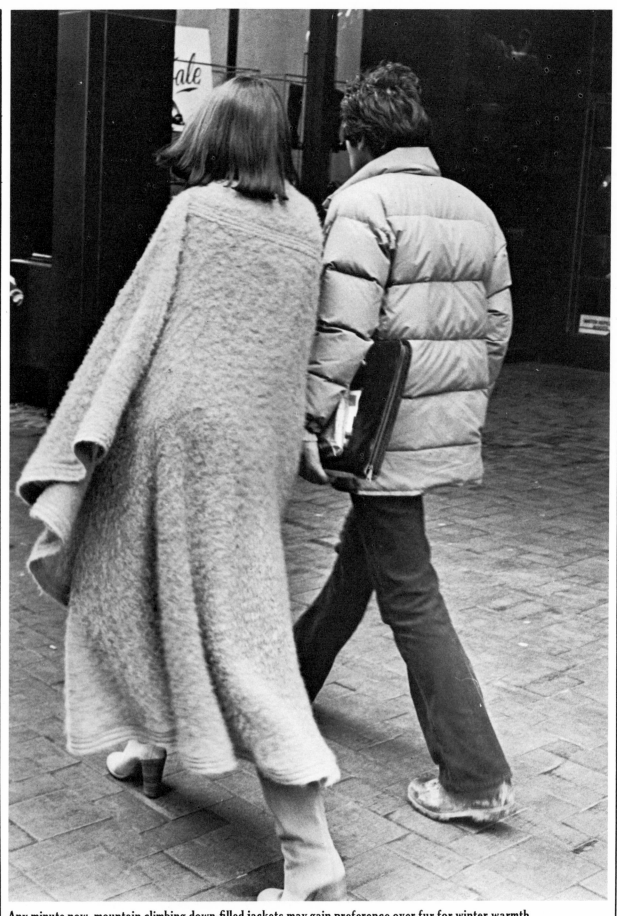

Any minute now, mountain climbing down-filled jackets may gain preference over fur for winter warmth.

Snowy flirting in stylish wools from the local sports store.

you are "molding your body to the terrain in a lyrical fashion. Freestyle is basically a feminine sport, intuitive and developmental, as opposed to pure, competitive, rational, aggressive male sports."

Of course, you can wear the uniforms of these aggressive male sports without competing, and if you're interested, here are a few team sports possibilities.

meanness, speed, and rebellion ever since Marlon Brando and the Hell's Angels. Leathers are particularly effective in black if you want to look tough! And they wear forever. A classic leather motorcycle jacket can take you through many cold winters in warmth and style—and if you happen to own a motorcycle, so much the better.

If you tire of black or brown, you can have a set of bright racing leathers custom-made by Bates in soft, thick leather with a zip-front jacket, contrasting zip sleeves, and black piping trim. To go full speed, get tight matching pants with a contrasting racing stripe up the side. It's hard for a motorist to miss you in Kawasaki green!

Ski clothes have always been very expensive; but behind the high prices lay good fabrics and excellent construction. Unless you live in a terribly cold climate, it is rather difficult to wear ski clothes as everyday wear except for the accessories like little knit caps and long johns. The beautifully stretchable one-piece ski outfits are like a second skin in freestyle skiing, where, according to Olympic skiier Suzy Chaffee,

Gracing the flats of snow in Sweden, Ewa Rudling skis cross-country like a pioneer. The old-fashioned ankle length wool skirt is romantic and locks in body heat too. 113

TEAM SPORTS

Team uniforms can be raided to yield colorful jerseys, knickers, shorts, socks, and mini beach covers. Use your imagination—combine Rollie Finger's socks with Walt Frazier's shorts and an Yves St. Laurent silk shirt (or even jockeys' silks)!

Basketball players wear great rayon jerseys with contrasting binding on a low-scooped neck and cut-in armholes, or sleeved versions with a contrasting neck and set-in sleeves. Either style is in a supple, silky weave. Some men think a cut-in basketball jersey makes a woman look like a jock. But that's their problem! Swimwear designers have picked up on basketball trunks and copied them for men's trunks. The originals are synthetic satin boxer shorts with wide, stretch waistbands and stripes around the bottom or up the sides. Why buy a French designer's "tap pants" when you can get basketball shorts that have twice as much sass?

Basketball socks have contrasting stripes mid-calf, and some are built to have a "self-stirrup," which means they look like a pair of baseball-style socks: the foot and heel are cut out over a pair of contrasting, full-foot socks.

Hockey has a violent aura. If you're feeling particularly mean someday, you might want to suit up in a hockey jersey with a classic lace-up neck, inset saddle shoulders, and long sleeves with a white stripe inset above the elbow. A rayon-cotton fabric

The quick feet of Pele, the most famous soccer player in the world, move with the speed of the Puma he wears.

gives the jersey a good combination of silkiness and absorption, and they're very effective as minidresses. Heavy cotton socks reach mid-thigh, with stirrups under the feet and wide stripes above the ankle. The pants themselves are unwearable. They're just a visual cover-up for side, tail, thigh, and crotch guards, an assemblage of pad pockets. But those socks are wonderful.

Football pants with the laced fly and web belts are nice in white duck, but like hockey pants they tend to be designed more for protective pads than for the body. Football jerseys are an American classic with their double shoulders and yokes, striped arms,

The padded shirt softens the blows of rugby.

and gusseted armpits, and they are long and loose enough for summer dresses. Small sizes from the boys' department are nice for layering. One of the new fabrics they come in is a nylon mesh knit.

The psychological importance of color in competitive clothes is seen in the old home-team rule—a high-school team playing on their home turf was allowed to wear white uniforms. They felt white made them appear gigantic to their opponents and gave them the winning edge.

Soccer is becoming more and more popular in the States. Although it's equally as bone crushing as football or hockey, soccer jerseys have lace-up necks, short or long sleeves with contrasting collars and stripes, short shorts, and brightly striped socks with turnover cuffs which pull over the knee on women. Rugby jerseys in cotton with drill collars and button-placket front openings are very sporty in solids or stripes. Goalie pants for soccer players come with padded hips. (If you want to look even more curvaceous in shorts, check out Frederick's of Hollywood's padded girdles!)

Baseball uniforms are made of several layers. The raglan-sleeved, braid-trimmed, cotton flannel top snaps over a baseball undershirt which has solid-color sleeves and a white body. The knicker-length pants are worn over high-cut, striped stirrup hose and contrasting inner socks. You should check out the layered socks. Add a snappy high-crowned baseball cap and everyone will get hungry for hot dogs, mustard and Beer Day at Wrigley Field.

Letter jackets are a traditional "civilian" counterpart to all this competitive regalia. Like *American Graffitti*, they epitomize the hot-rod era of the fifties and sixties. Sporting-goods supply stores that carry uniforms

Ali in training stays warm while seriously thinking.

Get healthier and happier jogging your way around the city or country as Sue Murray and Ingrid Boulting do.

Waiting for the right moment—leather clad, ready to go.

often carry letter jackets. They have been the rage in Paris for sometime now and sell for $100 over there. The classic letter jacket comes with leather sleeves and slash-pocket trim; a reprocessed wool body; stretchy striped collar, cuffs, and waist, and a snap front. If you don't want to spring for a jacket, a letter sweater is always stylish around the Beach Boys and the Dell Vikings. And a cheerleader's heavy sweater with crew neck is the cat's meow.

INDIVIDUAL SPORTS

Fencing jackets are usually too stiff to wear comfortably, but they have a unique, time-worn cut and come in pleasant cotton fabrics.

Judo is a more promising area for Cheap Chic: a judo ghi is made of pure cotton duck with a wrap front and dropped shoulders. We have seen them made in a diamond-quilted cotton duck with triple stitching on the sleeves. They look beautiful over soft white pants, but be careful about picking the color of the belt you wear! You don't want to get challenged on what you thought was merely a point of fashion.

Golf is the sport responsible for introducing those bright, bold colors into weekend sports clothes. Professional golfers like Carol Mann always look terrific in their bright mini golf skirts and matching tops, socks, and gloves. But that's because they have contracts with the manufacturers and can afford all the mix and match, since the clothes are free. Golf clothes are really rather difficult to put together with others, because the trim of the skirt is usually quite strong and demands a matching top. If you can't afford several sets of golf clothes, perhaps the best item from the golfer's repertoire is the visor, which looks especially striking over a crisp cotton scarf tied peasant-style at the back of the head. Golfers' fingerless gloves are rather interesting, and the classic fringed golfing shoes look beautiful (without the cleats) for city or country walks, sort of like saddle shoes with an extra spin on them.

If your self-image tends toward **hiking** into the sunset with a copy of *Field And Stream*, the L. L. Bean catalog from Freeport, Maine, is a must. They have everything from the puff-ball eiderdown ski jackets you see on every school kid to all the woodland fantasies: an Australian bush hat with built-in mosquito netting, Lees Frisco corduroy jeans, wading shoes, fishing jackets, hiking boots, rain suits, suede musette bags, leather and twill haversacks, and a virtual wonderland of roughing-it paraphernalia which translates perfectly to city living.

The personal twist that makes active sports clothes amusing to wear every day lies in taking them out of the context of their particular sport and customizing them to your whims. Mix a baseball shirt with a wide seersucker skirt and wrap it with a soft leather belt. Wear an oatmeal wool tunic over bright hockey socks and a turtleneck in the winter. Wear satin boxer shorts with nothing else. And put a tough but well-fitting leather motorcycle jacket over a skimpy silk Halston dress. Use these clothes with a certain disdain for their original function but an appreciation for their functional style, and they will inspire you to keep a lean, lithe, lanky body and an aura of nonchalant sexuality.

Parkas combined with multi-colored woolies conquer the cold of city streets or mountainsides, if need be.

HELENE DE BARCZA

College Clothes on $150 a Year

A college student on a tight budget, Helene has nevertheless managed to work up her own personal style. She's nineteen and a freshman at Hunter College in New York.

"There aren't as many jeans and boots around school as there used to be. I think people want to look nicer. So you see more espadrilles and longer skirts, dresses made of that Indian muslin with big belts around the waist.

"Since I only have a budget of about $150 for the school year, I have to be really careful with everything I buy. Most of my clothes are in solids; I have only a few stripes and prints. I wear a lot of boys' shirts, Eagle Brothers shirts from my old school uniform. I have six- and seven-year-old hand-me-down turtlenecks, a couple of sweaters that are two or three years old, lots of jeans from the army-surplus store and a longish dress I found at a department store for $20. But I always wear scarves, which makes things look special. A lot of my money went for my boots—the leather ones cost $60 and the denim ones were $30 at Chandler's. Then

I've got some leather espadrilles and a similar pair in cloth, and a pair of dressy shoes, but never for school.

"In the winter I wear this black thrift-shop skirt almost every day, with a shirt, a scarf around my neck, and a chain with little charms on it from friends. Or I'll wear jeans rolled up over my denim boots, a shirt with a thin sweater over it, and a scarf knotted at the neck.

"The black and Puerto Rican girls in school really pulled a look together that is sharp and very inexpensive. They'll wear earrings, a bracelet, a little hat, an inexpensive Indian cotton skirt, or rolled jeans with a thrift-shop jacket . . . and they look fabulous! It's not the budget, it's the imagination.

"On the weekends, I wear old school sweatpants with cowboy boots and a shirt. It's cheap, and it looks different!

"Sometimes I wish I had more money. I'd love to have clothes, but I don't want to own the same kind as the kids with money. Some of my things may look similar, but I think I always wear them differently."

ETHNIC

Ethnic clothes are in a certain disrepute these days. Lips curl at the mere sound of the word, and it's easy to understand why. Mass manufacturers have cheapened, bastardized, knocked off, diluted, and wrung the juice out of ethnic looks. And on top of all that, ethnic clothes have the gall to be bright and colorful in this depressed era of ours. But so what! Ethnic clothes can make you feel like a million bucks if you pick out the styles congenial to you. You can feel as if you're traveling to the Peruvian Andes as you set off for a business appointment; feel like you're off to a Hawaiian pig roast when you're actually en route to a leftover supper.

There's something about wearing a garment that's the product of another culture which is adventurous, even daring. If you have a beautiful printed silk kimono, for instance, you have to acclimate yourself to the bright, contrasting colors, to the sensual feel of the silk lining against your bare skin, the looseness of the sleeves and slit sides over a bare chest. You even have to move differently, because if you storm about a room in a normal Western way, your kimono will fall open. It gives you more body awareness—you quickly sense where your elbows are or you soon find the long, hanging arm of your kimono draped in the soup, in the salad, or up in flames.

The really special thing about ethnic

clothes is the fact that they are totally original. And when you blend in some exotic garment with your own well-worn and well-loved wardrobe, something interesting is bound to happen. (Just spend half an hour in your room with the radio blasting and start acquainting your new ethnic purchases with everything in your closet. You're sure to come up with a special look.) Ethnic clothes can be worn in a subtle way. They can be as classic as a tweed skirt if you think of them as individual garments rather than as parts of some exotic costume—if you take them out of context.

The trick of buying ethnic is to get a sense of the garment's inherent style and feel, independent of the rest of the outfit with which it's usually associated. Do with it what you will. Ethnic clothes seem to lose their vitality when foreign manufacturers move into a country and set up shop for mass-marketing designs that once had a very personal feel. After several years of these mass-manufactured imports, we have reached the point where we can select only the best. People are learning to look twice before they buy something with an ethnic air to it. It has to be a very special item; otherwise, you will be branded a hippy, and no one wants to look that dated! Selectivity pays off. In a few years, you won't be able to find true ethnic clothes anymore.

Sometimes it is easier to find national dress in the shops of America, like the Old Country stores along Clark Street in Chicago. A friend of ours was driving through Czechoslovakia several years ago and wanted to buy some typical Eastern European peasant scarves. There were none to be found in the bustling department stores of Prague. Yet, you can find them easily in New York. It seems that immigrant groups in the United States have held onto their national dress as a means of asserting their national identity; in the host country everyone rushes headlong into the future.

Lesley Jean Goldberg has made an art of the way she dresses, managing to put to-

The most elegant nomads of the Sahara desert are the Touareg tribe in Niger. Their loose robes, head wrappings, silver jewelry, embroidered money pouches and garments are all purchased at the market in Agades.

gether a very luxurious ethnic look without having the money to travel around the world. Lesley is an artist who works in soft sculpture, creating strange, attenuated people with looks of bland astonishment and plenty of sexual paraphernalia.

She assembled her beautiful wardrobe in San Francisco, where she haunted flea markets and used clothing shops, and cultivated friendships with the dealers who make trips to Africa, Asia, and the Near East. She has

Emmanuelle Khahn designed this graceful handkerchief skirt, the trim patiently embroidered by deft Roumanian artisans. Venitia finds it an ideal outfit for the squash court.

amassed so much jewelry that some hangs as decor in her house and the rest spills out of a big, beautiful Japanese mother-of-pearl chest. She has big, heavy Russian pieces, necklaces and coins, and silver and amber from Morocco, Ethiopia, Afghanistan, the Berbers, Turkomans . . . rare coral and enamels, carnelian, turquoise and jade rings, mammoth opalescent Dutch beads, African trade beads, Peking glass, ivory, carved blood-red cinnabar, bone and coral. She spends a lot of time at her collecting but pays very little for these very special pieces. She knows the value of things and has paid her dues learning where to get them.

Lesley has, she admits, more jewelry than clothes, but her favorite dresses carry out the ethnic style: a beautiful quilted-cotton Russian coat that she wears lining-out; a kimono found at a flea market that she re-cut into a loose V-necked dress because the edges were frayed. She loves soft silks and panne velvets, and when she's not wearing one of three extraordinary robes, Lesley puts her tops and dresses on over a long black velvet skirt and expensive boots, or mixes ethnic pieces with Victorian antiques. Lesley always looks like an exotic vision, a traveler back from Timbuktu loaded down with luxurious booty.

Martine Sitbon does travel. She says that dressing well is not a question of money. She doesn't buy ready-to-wear but looks for the special items that really please her. For about ten years she's dressed in old clothes from her grandmother's attic and thrift shops, but now she's turned her attention to antique ethnic clothes. "They're colorful and not sophisticated. I like a prophet look, large white Moses robes! I dream of Cecil B. DeMille movie clothes walking around, beautiful wool burnouses and big cotton djellabas. And I think makeup and kohl is important to accentuate a mood. I see it as an exaggeration, a kind of daily theatrics. Every day you wear a different mask. You put your mood on your face with makeup, and it, in turn, affects you and the people around you."

If you or one of your friends is about to take off on an exotic journey, here are a few observations and hints about the special finds you can discover while traveling.

Markets Around the World

Long before there were shopping centers and supermarkets, specialty stores and boutiques, goods were being traded in open or large covered markets. People gathered at regular intervals to buy, sell, trade, and gossip. The marketplace was the center of town as it still is in most country villages outside North America. Village markets in any country always seem to generate excitement. They are a feast for the eye as well as the place for cheap finds.

The first buy is a local **basket** or bag.

The Majorca/Ibiza straw basket is now an essential international summer carryall. Everyone who visits these islands off the Mediterranean coast of Spain buys one. The shape and flexibility of the basket are so practical that stores all over the world carry it as a steady item. In some countries the basket may turn out to be a net (like the *filet* in France), a knotted square of cotton from Japan, a stiff, round basket reinforced with metal shipping bands from Jamaica, or the goatskin bag of southern Morocco.

The natives of Bangladesh trade beads, bracelets, hand carved pipes and other goods at the markets.

Make sure to find a light basket for long-distance trekking.

Markets are usually divided into stalls, and most of the time you will find the fruits and vegetables in one area, the meat and fish in another, and then an area for clothes, kitchen utensils, and crafts. The fabric and clothing sections are very different from market to market, depending on the abilities, ingenuity, and needs of the local people.

Each country and each province within that country has a set of traditions and clothes which by now take a trained eye to spot, since the whole world is becoming increasingly Westernized. People who like unusual clothes are quick to discover the find that is not imported at an enormous markup. Clothing sold at the marketplace may look attractive and colorful to the foreign eye, but it is there primarily because it is functional, durable, cheap, and usually made of local raw materials.

What to Look for in

EUROPE

Europe is the Old Country where fabric and color know-how originated. To learn how to recognize quality sweaters, for instance, step into a truly British shop and finger all the cashmere sweaters until you appreciate the difference between synthetics and the finest of wools. In France, Switzerland, and Italy, buy a yard or two of the most luxurious fabrics—crepe de Chine, georgette, or peau de soie—make a shift or wear it as a head scarf. If possible, always buy fabrics in the country of origin, where you get the advantage of local prices.

BRITAIN is famous for its quality sweaters. Shetland and lambs' wool can be found all over the country in chain stores and Woolworths at decent prices. Tweeds at all price levels are also a perennial item, particularly in Scotland, where weavers have a way of blending earthy colors that take your imagination back to the highlands. In Scotland the multitude of clan plaids sell by the kilt or by the yard.

IRELAND knits some of the warmest white wool sweaters on any side of the Atlantic Ocean. They are worn by everyone, whether they work the land, do office work, or simply pub crawl in Dublin. These sweaters are also perfect for the ski slopes of the Alps and Colorado, wintry campuses, and city streets.

SCANDINAVIA has all the best local clothes in the back country. The northern countries still have a strong folklore tradition which keeps local costumes dancing through the villages. In Norway, Sweden, and Finland, the country women wear white embroidered shirts with wide, embroidered, handwoven wool skirts over petticoats. They usually add a white apron and a bonnet (which we can do without today), but the tight, little, laced-up bolero completing the outfit is appealing. New ones can be found in the general stores and at local dressmakers, used ones in the secondhand shops. In Norway the best buys are the colorful sweaters with plain backgrounds and geometric patterns that start at the neck and expand toward the chest. They are sold as cardigans or crew necks, and if you have the time, they can be knitted for you in your own choice of colors if you can find a willing pair of hands.

Sweden excels in contemporary sports clothes, found in most of their department stores. There is a Swedish army coat which strikes many men visitors as being very practical. It's white canvas lined with sheepskin, with large pockets, and is cut, like all military clothes, with great classic proportions. The Swedish army coat can be found used in surplus stores or made new for a reasonable price at any military tailor. It looks good soiled, but if you like it white, wash it often in lukewarm water and let it dry away from direct heat.

GERMANY makes sturdy and efficient items without frivolities. The styles are often stiff, the colors muddy. Walking shoes are strong and well-made, but the Germanic forté is leather—coats and jackets that last a lifetime.

HOLLAND has its share of sailors' outfits, and Amsterdam has a "thieves' market" (or flea market) with a lot of good antique clothing.

BELGIUM: In no other place in the world are the women so agile with their fingers as the lacemakers in Ghent. Try replacing a worn collar with a dash of exquisite Belgian lace, or buy it by the yard to blend with other fabrics for a dress.

FRANCE, like the rest of Europe, has great local weekly markets where you can find things not sold in stores: slippers, wooden clogs with straw outside and sheepskin inside, large calico aprons, peasant blouses, long cotton underwear, head scarves, and fabrics that reflect the temperature of the region. Brittany has lots of rain; therefore you can be sure to find good sailors' raincoats and navy sweaters. The Riviera basks in the sun and produces the tiniest, best-cut bikinis in the world, as well as a whole array of light cotton sportswear in warm colors. Markets, small shoe stores, and department stores all carry the marvelous walking shoe known as "l'espadrille." It originated as a peasant shoe made with a canvas top and a light flexible straw from Algeria, ideal for weaving into a most comfortable sole.

French people have a knack for redesigning functional wear into appealing, must-have-it-in-your-wardrobe pieces of clothing. The espadrille became the most sensible footwear to own for men, women, and children. At first you could buy it only with a flat sole. Then Yves St. Laurent spotted a Basque shop near his first ready-to-wear store which handmade the shoes with an elevated wedge and laces to tie around the ankles. He contracted the Basque workshop to turn them out exclusively for his boutique. Flowers were embroidered on the canvas, and the colors became wilder until everyone caught on that the espadrille with an elevated heel was really the happiest and most comfortable shoe around. Now they are manufactured throughout the United States and Europe in a great variety of shapes and sizes. Chances are that you will not find a cheaper shoe except for the weird, functional sandal known as the "shrimping sandal," made of molded plastic.

SPAIN AND PORTUGAL both are a delight for people who have the patience and imagination to have their clothes custom-made. Ask around and someone is bound to recommend a good seamstress who will copy your favorite old shirt or whip up a skirt with hand finishing in the exact style you desire. Madrid was once famous for its suede and soft-leather shops that could custom-tailor anything you wanted in a few days. Now, as foreign manufacturers monopolize the market, there seem to be fewer shops like these. Yet the quality, color, and fit of the work of the small workshops and craftsmen found in Spain are very rewarding for people who love the feel of suede and leather. The Barrio Chino in Barcelona has the strongest boots (inspired by Frye) for a mere $25.00. In Majorca, ingenious cobblers make custom boots and shoes. Ordinary lace-up boots can be specially made with a small patch of Moroccan carpeting. If this costs more than your purse can afford, you can always pick up the best Spanish walking shoes—part canvas, part suede, with a sole made from recycled tires. Several people we know have been wearing them for four years or more. Pollensa in Majorca is one of the towns that specializes in this shoe. A similar style of sandal, locally called "Tijuana retreads," is available throughout the American Southwest at a very modest price.

ITALY is also crazy for shoes. There are shoe stores on every corner, and even the cheapest have great styles and colors, particularly in Milan. There seems to be more emphasis on men's wear in Italy. Good, cheap, and stylish suits can be found in many department stores.

CZECHOSLOVAKIA, HUNGARY, RUMANIA, AND POLAND are the places to look for hand embroidery on white cloth, meticulously sewn by diligent female hands. The tradition of hand embroidery began for filling trousseaus, but today these beautiful peasant clothes can be purchased in government stores and tourist shops.

YUGOSLAVIA still has a lot of folk crafts at fairly cheap prices which the local people take for granted. A good selection can be found in folklore stores and high-class souvenir shops similar to the shops in New York's East Village. These stores carry jewelry, costumes, luggage, and assorted crafts brought in by the peasants on market day. Farmers come from the villages surrounding the cities with sacks of knit socks, sandals woven from leather strips, vegetables, and cheeses for sale or trade. Mixed with all these goods are beautifully embroidered robes and intricate filigree bracelets that they regard as mere old clothing and trinkets. Bartering and trading between visitor and peasant is quite popular, especially when done with a smile and for the pleasure of the exchange.

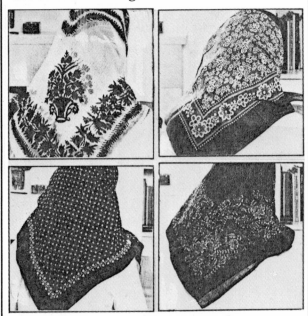

Large cotton muslin peasant scarves can be worn many ways: babushka style, wrapped as a turban, tied as a halter or beach skirt. From Greece or Greek stores.

GREECE has, from time immemorial, seen its people dressed in shirts and dresses made from the off-white gauze that is woven on the islands. In the days of Socrates, the cloth was worn as a toga, and today it seems that summer clothes are returning to these loose, comfortable styles. Once again the mills are weaving the white cloth that is so perfect for wrapping and draping. After you have covered your body, choose an open pair of sandals which slip around your toe. The Greeks really know how to make sandals that last, as well as using the prettiest colors for decoration. Jewelry found in Greece is particularly attractive and can run from the simple bronze cross of Mikonos to the bright blue glass beads taken from donkeys' saddles and strung into necklaces.

Russian peasant clothes: the woman's dress of the Ryazan province; the man's traveling coat is from central Russia.

RUSSIA is one of the few countries where amber is in abundance. Necklaces, bracelets, and rings can be purchased very reasonably at Beryoskas in the government shops catering to tourists who will pay in foreign currency. Another sound buy is the Chapka, that famous Russian hat with the ear flaps. Made of mink tails, fox, astrakhan, or rabbit fur, they will keep any head warm even in the coldest of Siberian winters. If you do go as far as Siberia, track down the secondhand shops—with luck you may find a local policeman's sheepskin coat in off white or brown. The superb tailoring, the fitted chest, and large collar make them very special.

The most Russian of all garments is the side-fastening, collarless, bloused shirt worn in khaki wool by the army and in beige/brown by the country people. The festive version of these shirts is made in white or black satin with embroidered ribbons at the cuff and neck, held loosely at the waist with a wide leather belt or a simple cord. The image of traditional Russia is that of a country woman wearing a long jacket over a loose dress with heavy boots, her head covered with a babushka or floral scarf of wool challis with pink and red roses mingled in among green leaves.

AFRICA

This is a continent where you can sit for hours at the marketplace with the robe maker and discuss at length the blue of a cloth, the zigzag designs his machine can perform, and describe what you want for yourself by indicating what you like on the people passing by. Most of the population in countries like Algeria, Morocco, Tunisia, Mali, Niger, and Egypt have been wearing the same basic type of clothing for the past two thousand years: pre–New Testament classics such as woven woolen capes that double as blankets, gabardine caftans, and large cotton robes for both men and women.

NORTH AFRICA is one of the least bastardized of all regions as far as clothes are concerned. The *souk* is the old open market of the large towns. You're well advised to take one of those self-appointed guides that crowd the entrance, because the place is like a labyrinth. These guides are usually young boys full of tricks and enthusiasm. Select the calmest one you can find since they can drive you crazy trying to make dizzy deals with their store-owner companions (to whom they will no doubt lead you at triple speed). You can wander in alone, but you'll find that all along the way young boys will walk alongside of you whether you like it or not. Once you see

These Moroccan women adorn themselves with their finest amber and silver jewelry. The huge, inlaid metal triangles add beauty but also secure veil and robe against the mountain winds. Silver kohl accents their eyes.

Moroccan men still dress as in biblical times.

something you really want, you might as well get it right there, because you are going to see hundreds that look pretty much alike, and the few pennies you might bargain down are not worth the energy. Or, you can choose your cloth and trimmings for a *djellaba* (a long house robe) and go over all the details with the tailor: length of sleeve, side slits, etc. All this usually takes place over a cup of sweet mint tea. Shopping in Arab countries is considered an agreeable pastime; you meet, sit, chat, and exchange views. It is not an impersonal

A blend of ethnic sources. His Tibetan cotton shirt and white jeans are almost a uniform. Her favorite house dress is this white cotton robe stitched together in the souks of Marrakech one day for a mere ten dollars.

supermarket or department-store operation where you dash in, grab, pay, and dash out.

EQUATORIAL AFRICA has body coverings, for the bush and cities alike, that are even more basic. The wide, loose shirts for men let the air through and can be bought at the market in a great variety of prints. The women wrap their heads with a large piece of cotton batik and wrap their bodies from bosom to ankles in a similar print. At the market you can get typically colorful African batiks with cameos of the local president or the late President Kennedy, General de Gaulle, and other political personalities.

In any country, check what the local people are wearing on their feet; it's usually the cheapest and most durable regional footwear. In this part of the world shoes are called *samsaras*, and can be found at the stall of the man in charge of leather at the general market. The same vendor will also have leather pouches worn around the neck or diagonally across the chest, which serve as a money purse for both men and women. These hand-sized pouches are worked in different-colored leathers and have many concealed compartments to store amulets, money, medicinal herbs, and photographs.

Venetian beads used centuries ago as bartering pieces, and no longer available in Venice, pile up in little mounds of swirling colors among the heavy silver bracelets in the alleyways. The blanket vendors sell carefully woven narrow strips stitched together to form assorted-sized blankets with geometric patterns and dazzling colors. If you arrive early at the bush or city market, you can get everything at almost half price —a friendship discount. Ideally, one should not require any other entertainment, because the open markets are so fantastic. As the heart and life of any region, they give you a real feeling for the country. In Nigeria and Ghana the heavy-work laborers wear a cotton patchwork sleeveless tunic that sells for less than 50¢.

All over Africa, the most venerated man next to the local chief and the medicine man is the blacksmith. He not only makes horseshoes but also fashions silver jewelry out of coins by melting and casting them in sand.

Henna-mud designs, lasting for two weeks to a month, both decorate and antisepticize. These designs took an entire day of skillful and ancient craftsmanship.

In Agades, Niger, we saw a European woman, amazed at the timeless, precise work of the blacksmith, give him one of her favorite Navajo bracelets to copy. The result was all the more interesting since it combined two very distinct and distant cultures.

A great part of the Niger population consists of the Tuareg or "blue people," who wrap their heads in a navy blue fabric that looks like carbon paper. The color from the fabric rubs off on their heads, which is the reason why they are called blue people. They are a nomadic tribe who roam the area carrying goods to inaccessible regions. A rugged people, they have for centuries worn loose, wide robes and turbans to resist heat, wind, and sand. The women gracefully wrap yardage of azure blue cloth above a long robe of white lace. When they have children, the long robe is cut at the waist so the baby can be breast fed. These people have become such masters at artfully using fabric that during the dawn dance they manage to make their headgear resemble a cock's comb, the animal they want to imitate.

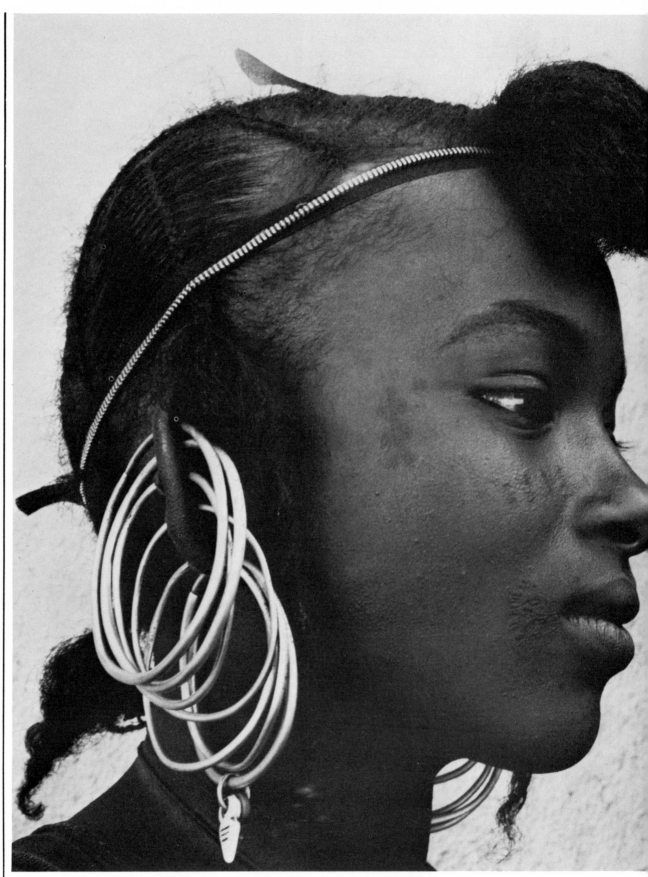

Cheap chic in the middle of the Sahel region! This Fulani nomad, a goat herder, adorns her braided hair with one side of a long black and gold zipper. The number of simple metal loops represents wealth in livestock.

Ever wondered what the faces behind Arab veils look like? Azebu, an Algerian, dresses in the traditional layers of cotton. First a sarousal (loose pantaloons), then a long flowered chemise and dark blue veil topped by white netting.

Another nomadic tribe of that country are the Fulani. The men and women wear little pouches around their necks that contain small mirrors and a pair of tweezers to remove both the thorns from their feet and the hair from their foreheads and beards.

All over Africa, there is an endless variety of beadwork and the use of grass or straw for skirts, hats, and bags. Besides the marketplace, there are talented craftspeople who work in small huts tucked away in villages. If you can express what it is you are looking for, the local people will lead you to the artisans.

THE MIDDLE EAST

This area has a very limited selection of women's wear, except for the big white sheet exposing only one eye. (But you just might go for an Arafat type of head wrap.) Men are equally uniformed, in their long white robes and muslin turbans.

TURKEY has deep red velvet jackets and dresses which have gotten even better with age. They are often embroidered with gold or silver threads and can be retrieved from masses of smelly clothes in Ali Baba-type secondhand shops. Turkey is also well known for beautiful silver belts which, depending on the source and workmanship, run from about $40 to $300. Local shops in Istanbul and in many little villages display crinkled cotton shirts in a natural egg-shell color, with or without red stripes. The same garment can be found in knee or ankle length and are all very cheap.

JORDAN AND ISRAEL have the Bedouin woman's dress with the embroidered yoke, one of the most sensible long robes on earth. It comes in either heavy cotton or black velvet and is tucked under the breast all the way to the waist. When a woman reaches the middle of a pregnancy, it is untucked for extra room.

PAKISTAN AND AFGHANISTAN have been over-exploited for their mirror-embroidered

Baby stays snug in this little Afghanistan mirrored coat straight from the market-place in the mountains.

skirts and shirts, and the strong-smelling goatskin coats. Yet the women who live in the northern regions wear a type of clothing very different from that seen in the south. They are difficult to see because the women hide themselves behind a black veil with only a net insert at eye level, but underneath they wear large black cotton dresses with silver embroidery of great beauty, worn with heavy silver bangles. If you love boots and want to have a pair made that will be inexpensive but very special, see the cobblers of Afghanistan, who work in leather and make soft riding boots that can be ordered with or without embroidery.

INDIA has such a huge selection of cheap clothes that one really has to examine carefully before buying. The rush was so great on all the long cotton skirts, vests, Nehru type shirts and such that little attention was given to the quality of the stitching or the cut. However, the people of India who still care produce some of the finest clothes such as the very popular *kurta* (white voile shirts with simple drawstring pants). Each province of India has an individual style—the state of Baroda, the state of Madras, and so on, each with particular colors and prints for the saris in which the women wrap themselves.

KASHMIR, the fertile and lush valley at the top of India, is a paradise for market lovers. It is the kingdom of papier-mâché—beautiful jewelry and jewelry boxes, painted with intricate miniature floral designs and then varnished to sparkle in the sun. Fur coats abound, but again, if you have one made, select the skins with someone who is knowl-

edgeable. The hides should be supple, the fur shiny. Work closely with the tailor so that the seams are not half done with weak thread and the length is correct, as Americans in general are considerably taller than the local inhabitants. Wolf, fox, and other skins can be made into coats for about $100. Embroidered shawls made of the finest wools come in subtle shades and are covered with hand-stitched paisley designs.

NEPAL, the small country that begins where India rises to meet the Himalaya Mountains, has quilted coats of heavy hand-woven fabrics that can be dyed and/or made to order. People there have a wonderfully unique way of layering colorful woolen garments when the cold sets in.

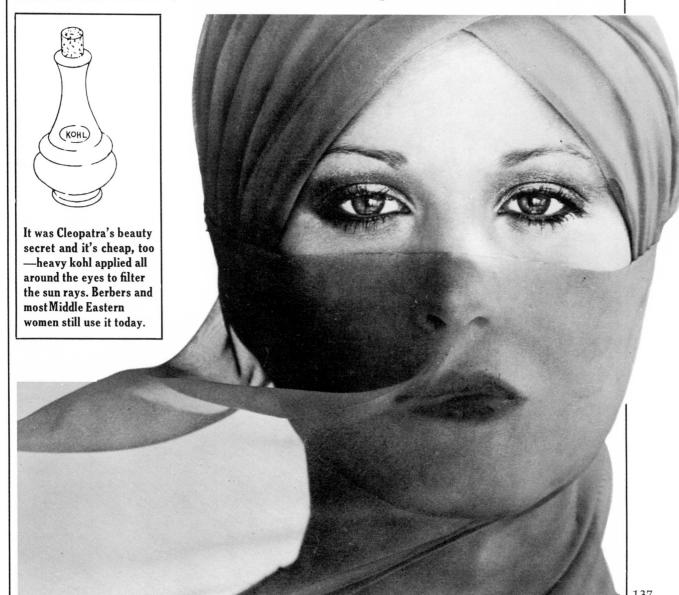

It was Cleopatra's beauty secret and it's cheap, too —heavy kohl applied all around the eyes to filter the sun rays. Berbers and most Middle Eastern women still use it today.

137

ASIA

As you will discover in the wrapping chapter, INDONESIA has developed maximum simplification in its clothes. Men and women wear a sarong or length of waxed batik wrapped around the hips as a long skirt. For women it is topped with a sheer voile, loose blouse edged with flower embroidery.

In BALI, the graceful and magical island, the young boys walk along the beaches with dried seaweed bracelets, delicate shell necklaces, and tortoiseshell rings. To find the best bargains in batiks, go deep into the market, as the peripheral vendors are out to get the hurried tourist for as much as they can. (For those who like pipes, the Balinese are also great carvers of ebony or bone pipes, chiseled with great love and artistry.)

VIETNAM may not be a place you might think of to explore in search of Cheap Chic. But if you look at the Vietnamese women, so delicate and elegant in their long, narrow, satin dresses worn over pants, you may be tempted to wear one too. They are available, ready-made, in most Vietnamese clothing shops in Paris.

CAMBODIA has black satin sarongs with embossed flowers so subtle they can hardly be seen. (Silk from Thailand is plentiful and beautiful, but tends to be too shiny and expensive to be considered Cheap Chic.) Along the market stalls and in various small shops around the country, silver and gold are sold by the ounce. Simple silver belts are sold by weight. The decorated links are fashioned in such a way that they can fit any size waist or hips. Hopefully we will be able to travel again through this lovely country in the near future.

The Chinese influence on European dress is spreading fast. Stylish Parisian Sofi Bollack picked out this old black and gold brocade and had it transformed into a classic coat-dress.

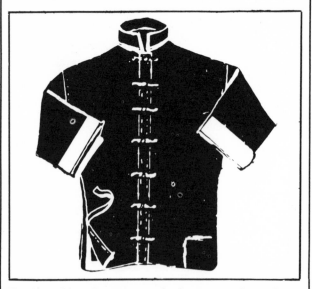

This basic kung-fu attire can also be an everyday jacket.

HONG KONG, Taiwan's neighbor, requires looking beyond the typical tourist traps to discover the really cheap and useful finds. There is a five-story building on the main street of the island called the China Emporium which sells a great assortment of quality goods made in mainland China. It is an outlet for them to collect foreign currency, and the prices on most things are ex-

Japanese students wear zoris with their traditional school uniforms.

A dazzlingly unique party style: knife, belt, and kimono!

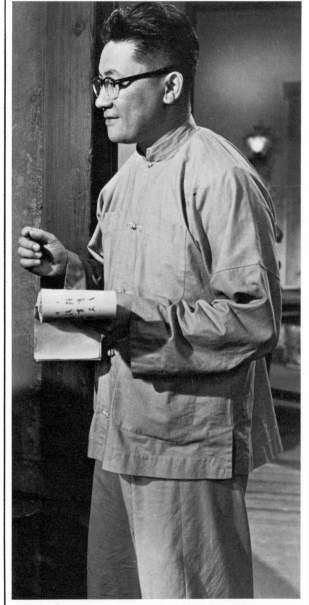

A most comfortable and universal garment: cotton pajamas. Both men and women can enjoy these loose simple clothes. Available in many colors besides the "people's blue," with handy pockets, they can be found in Chinese stores.

tremely reasonable. A friend of ours bought a backpack embroidered with funny animals which was a solid combination of silk and cotton. For her boyfriend, she brought back a navy blue quilted jacket which is as warm as a fur coat.

The "Chinese blues" are everywhere, of course. Both men and women wear those loose pants and straight jackets with frog fastenings. Depending on your inclination, you can get them either ready-made there or in any Chinatown in your own country. In Hong Kong you can pick up a smooth navy blue velvet jacket with silk lining and give it to a local tailor, who will quilt and custom finish it with special frogs in just a few days for about the same price as a jean's jacket and dungarees at home.

In China the regime of Mao brought about a sobriety in fashion which is very much in line with the Cheap Chic utilitarian idea. Yet there is a great deal of beauty and charm in the ancient Chinese robes, long skirts, and pajamas that are still worn today by older people in Hong Kong, Taiwan, and Chinese communities abroad. The amazing fact is that a lot of these decorated coat dresses can still be purchased at reasonable prices all over the world; they make most attractive at-home or party wear.

JAPAN

JAPAN is a treasure trove for anyone who appreciates refinement and delicacy in color and print. All the energy concerning clothes has gone into the same basic form for hundreds of years, the kimono. The only difference in kimonos lies in the fabric. The very formal way for a Japanese woman to dress is first to wear a knee-length white cotton kimono belted loosely with a length of dyed silk. On top of that goes a kimono of thin silk or rayon in a pastel color (usually printed with cherry blossoms) tied with an even more elaborate sash, then the final kimono of a color and embroidery dictated by the occasion. The formal kimono is truly an art form in itself, with paintings depicting an aspect of nature stitched in a world of glori-

Japanese designer Kansai Yamamoto's dramatic cape.

yukata is the most accessible and practical kimono. It is worn by the Japanese either at home or for traveling to and from the bath house. It usually comes in white cotton printed with natural or abstract motifs in navy blue or mauve. In a spa town you will see everyone walking around in these robes, and it is a refreshing sight. The *yukata* can be purchased for about $10 in any Japanese department store or for slightly more in the Japanese stores in our country.

A variation of these house kimonos is the *hoppi* coat, most often seen in black with a good-luck symbol or dragon on the back. Another very practical Japanese invention are *zoris*, or thong sandals, which come in every form—flat, on stilts, with straw soles, with a cork platform, with velvet or plastic padding. The *tabi*, or white cotton foot covering that fastens on the side, completes the traditional wear. It is fairly inexpensive, but not very practical. Nippon ingenuity also includes beautiful but cheap waxed paper umbrellas priced so that you don't mind losing it.

ously colored threads. The large sash or *hobi* securing the top kimono is carefully considered and almost as costly as the kimono because of the handwoven brocade from which it is made.

For everyday wear, the outer kimono for both men and women is of a flat woven cotton or wool in earthy tones, often with a geometric pattern discreetly running through the fabric. For our money, the

A Nippon oil-paper umbrella serves well in America to protect this southern belle from the sun.

SOUTH AMERICA

Throughout South America there is a general feeling for simple hand-woven cloth that has multiple uses. The Indians turn out the most interesting combinations of colors and textures.

MEXICO, the sad and singing country that touches its white cotton clothes with vibrant colors, still produces a lot of attractive, cheap clothing. The market of Toluca, not far from Mexico City, sells a huge assortment of shiny, multicolored scarves.

Natural cotton is egg-shell colored. The shirts of this material that most men wear on Sundays in the villages are sold in the markets. They have long sleeves, narrow

This Mexican jacket of embroidered white wool goes for $25 in Paris, which is probably triple its price in Mexico.

pleats, and tiny bone or plastic buttons. In the south of Mexico, where it gets hotter, women's dresses are looser, like chemises, with large flowers embroidered on the shoulder straps and front to resemble big necklaces. Walking for long distances in the dusty heat is a part of life there, and the famous *huaraches*, leather-strip sandals, developed out of that need. Their flexibility and airiness have also made them very popular abroad.

Each country in South America has its distinct, almost national, sweater. In Mexico, the most appealing and classic is of thick natural wool with a shawl collar that comes up to your ears to protect your neck from the cold at night. Silver jewelry is cheap and looks it, but it is fun and imaginative. There are all sorts of brooches in butterfly or bird shapes, outlined in silver and inlaid with iridescent abalone shells, and small perfume bottles covered with cut-out silver flowers that let you see the remaining level of the liquid. You may find a *mariachi* leather belt studded with shiny nails, or an armadillo bag, which is both a curious and rather sad object.

GUATEMALA follows much the same line of clothing as its Mexican neighbor, except that the ponchos and shawls are even more common and often become a skirt, a scarf, or a head wrap at the twist of a wrist. You'll discover that each town has its own distinct weaving colors.

BRAZIL is so widespread and varied that it is difficult to pinpoint the many local specialties. The general markets are called *feiras*. In the cities they move to a different section every day. In the beach towns like Rio, you can purchase mercerized cotton thread at one stand, hand it over to be crocheted at the next stand, and have a bikini the next day for approximately $8. As an alternative to T-shirts, you can get some of those skimpy, spaghetti-strapped undershirts; they are made of cotton and take well to dyeing. A tougher look is that of the *cangaceiros*, the cowboys of Brazil, who wear all-leather chaps and tight jackets worn with wide sombrero hats. The saddle makers also produce large bags of different kinds of

leathers. The prettiest and least expensive hot-weather clothes come from the region of Bahia. Men of all ages wear white cotton trousers and loose white blouses in the Macumba region. Women's skirts are long, extremely wide, and often trimmed with lace.

People in Brazil pay a great deal of attention to superstition, and many will carry a few charms to ward off evil spirits. The most popular one is the *figa*, a carved hand with the thumb stuck between the index and the next finger. You can find them for very little money, made out of the semi-precious stones that abound in Brazil.

The Amazon Indians have a way of weaving fine straw and dyeing feathers to create tickly necklaces. They also alternate beans, dipped in earthy colors, with little stones and tinted feathers, as is done nowhere else in the world.

More booty from Mexico is this handpainted sequined skirt. Only sixteen dollars across the border!
Right, The South American Mix: A Mexican blanket skirt, Bolivian sweater and a coat from a Peruvian poncho.

146

Bolivia and Peru have very colorful ponchos, gloves, and bonnets, knit with childlike designs, which keep the mountaineers warm and free in their movement. Whenever a traveler starts talking about the markets of South America, the conversation always comes back to the multitude of patterns in weaving. It is also an amazing sight to see women at the market wearing hats that closely resemble bowlers or businessmen's hats.

Of course, you don't need all of these things we have discussed, since you are not going to find yourself in all these places at the same time anyway. But if you do find yourself living in any of these places, you will begin to realize that coverings are made to suit the life of a particular region. If you adapt local clothing comfortably to your own needs, you will probably wear it for a long time to come. People who are knowl-edgeable about clothes end up with a few things that they wear over and over again, instead of constantly changing simply for effect. Clothes help create your mood for having a good day. When the magic of a particular style or combination has worn out, move on to another which refreshes your whole outlook.

In any country around the world, the marketplace is really the first place to visit to get a feel for the people. Chances are that you will find exactly what you need to wear right there. Why not try traveling without any luggage, and clothe yourself completely in local costumes?

A final word of caution: For most of the clothes we have talked about, a gentle lukewarm hand washing or the dry cleaners is the best cleaning method. Most wools and cottons used in these countries are not pre-shrunk, so they will either fade or shrink one or two sizes in the washing machine.

Tiny strips of cotton are folded, appliqued and made into this unusual jacket by Florida Indians.

147

Heavy sweaters, like this Peruvian one, can warm you year round.

If you are not a traveler, you can find plenty of ethnic clothing in the United States. American Indians have a folklore that is rich in tradition and readily available on the home front. Yet the ethnic clothing of the American Indian also travels well abroad. Nicolas Harle, a friend of ours in France, has taken the Indian tradition to Paris. His first inspiration came from a book called *Indian Crafts and Lore: How to Live Like an Indian*, by Ben Hunt, which tells how to make clothes, jewelry, hairstyles, and sand paintings. "I was so fascinated that I made myself a pair of leather trapper pants," says Nicolas, "there was nowhere that I could find them. Then Keith Richard and Anita Pallenberg saw them and asked me to make them some. That's how my Indian business started. I went on to fringed leather vests and jackets, all hand sewn. I bought Zuni and Navajo jewelry by mail order for next to nothing. In New York I ended up at an Indian trading post called Plume, where they have all the different feathers and skins and beads used by the different tribes, and I decided to open an 'Indian trading post' in Paris, which is the name of my shop.

"The least expensive things in my shop are adapted from the classic Indian wear: Kickapoo shirts, Navajo skirts, and coats made from Hudson's Bay blankets. The least expensive leathers are chamois. T-shirts run about $30. Deerskin pants run $80. My clientele ranges from pop stars to messenger boys, because I keep my prices reasonable. My adaptations please the Indian fanatics and seduce people who are looking for something personal. My next project is to make kits with the skins, leathers, threads of leather, patterns, and instructions so people with little money can have fun and make their own clothes."

With these basics tucked in your bag, you can travel wherever you like for as long as you like and always look sharp.

Serafine's straw hat was twenty-five cents in a Bahamas' market. The rest of her outfit was inexpensive too!

LARRY LeGASPI

Spacey Designs for Future Shock

Larry LeGaspi works out of Moonstone, a small design studio in the Village. His influence, however, is far wider. The incredible, soulful LaBelle flashed his space clothes all over the world, from Soul Train to Paris, from the Continental Baths to the Metropolitan Opera. The silver breasts which flashed off their costumes at the Met were made by Larry's partner, Richard Erker, who works with him on all their spacey silver jewelry. Some weeks, when a show is about to go on, Larry doesn't get to sleep until five or six in the morning.

"My design ideas come from my childhood fantasies. I dream of other planets. I'm always finding myself in very strange places in my imagination! The other night I had this dream of climbing up a cliff behind some sort of insect people. They had these incredible legs, or boots, and I woke up to sketch out the image for an idea.

"Space seemed the only direction for me to go, because the seventies just seem to be a repeat of the thirties through the sixties. I see my work as a kind of 'Space Deco.' I'm trying to get a lot of fluidity in the skirts and cutting the jersey on a bias, but I think the Deco look should have more of the future in it.

"I didn't decide I was going to do futuristic clothes until I went to Nepal two years ago. Before that, I was seeing things in a very contemporary way, very merchandisable, commercial. Then I said, 'Let's see if I can go one step further.' I started mixing the simple, clean line with the detail of trapunto at the neck or wrist. Now I find I can do anything with it.

"Half my customers are entertainers. My clothes are mainly for performers, because people are going to turn around and look at you in these things. Last week, I got stopped by the police for stopping traffic in my white leather and fur coat!"

150

WRAPPINGS

Wrapping the body is the simplest form of clothing and the most sophisticated. Some people consider the clothes of classic Greece to be the height of elegance. Today, millions of people around the world wear pieces of cloth draped and knotted and folded about the body. In Southeast Asia, men and women wear identical sarongs. In Africa, Masai tribesmen throw a large piece of orange cloth over their shoulders like a dashing cape. Desert robes and intricate turbans protect the Arabs from heat, wind, and sand. On the Indian continent, women wear a long length of fabric wrapped about their body, a sari. In South America, Indians only twenty miles from large cities still wear the simple loincloth. In America, Zuni women wrap fabric into skirts.

The art of keeping a piece of fabric on your body shows in the way you pull it, tie it, and work with the tucks and folds and bias . . . there are no buttons or zippers. For those of us who grew up knowing nothing but fastenings and more fastenings—zips, buttons, hooks, eyes, snaps, and laces—it

All it takes to gift-wrap yourself is a certain assurance about preventing that piece of fabric from slipping off your body. Christiana's discovery is to make a triangle out of a large Indian silk scarf, then with the long edge up, cross it in back and knot the points in front. Add a silver belt to determine the waistline, a whisp of point d'esprit tulle at the neck for drama and you have ingenious evening wear for next to nothing.

may be rather difficult to relax wearing just a flimsy piece of fabric wrapped between our bodies and the cold, cold world. But once you start playing with the idea of wrappings, it can become very exciting. All you have to work with is:

The fabric
The body
Your imagination

A combination of these three things can become the most sensual thing ever! What painting is more sumptuous than Ingre's *Turkish Bath*? How sparse it would look without the full, intricately wrapped turbans on the heads of the naked bathers. Draped fabric offers a soft, charming look in this world of stiffness and neatness.

Wrap up a skirt and halter, if you find yourself really down and out. You'll be back on top of the world looking totally unique. No one will mix patterns and colors the way you do, no one is going to wrap their body just the way you do, and no one has a

For a sexy summer skirt, take a large fringed shawl, hug it tight around the hips and knot it below the belly-button. If the fabric is slippery, add a safety pin underneath for security (and peace of mind).

A sarong is traditional for men in Southeast Asia. It's as simple as a wrap around the hips, pull and tuck.

Acetate or silky jersey lends itself best to elegant wrapping. A skirt is a twist of the fabric and a tuck at the hip. Or use long yardage and invent variations on the same theme: Slip one end between the legs, shaping a halter top and strapless pantaloons.

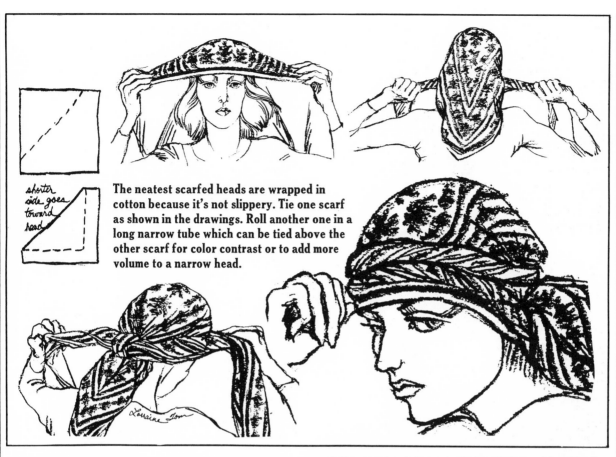

The neatest scarfed heads are wrapped in cotton because it's not slippery. Tie one scarf as shown in the drawings. Roll another one in a long narrow tube which can be tied above the other scarf for color contrast or to add more volume to a narrow head.

shorter side goes toward head

Starting with the same length of fabric, two very different looks in head coverings: At left, Ramona let Giorgio di Sant'Angelo invent an elegant double-twisted chignon, while the woman at right wears it dashiki style.

During her pregnancy, Marcia found the most comfortable covering around the house was a loosely held length of sari.

body to reveal that is quite like yours. You can't make a mistake. Wrapping is totally individual.

A girl who lives in Los Angeles makes full use of the warm weather—she pulls a long piece of peach jersey out of her drawer, wraps it once or twice around her body, plays with it this way and that, and finally settles on one style of draped gown for the evening. She has a talent for it, yes, but it's something we can all develop.

If you grow fond of this gentle, feminine look, you can buy yards and yards of silky jersey, Indian cotton muslin, antique scarves, Liberty of London prints, Provençal cottons, and Balinese saris; fabrics that stick to the body and don't slide around.

When you travel, pack a few folded lengths of fabric to soften modern motel lamps, change the color of the lighting, cover ugly bedspreads, hang as wispy curtains, and double up as beach towels and bikini covers. A few pieces of fabric can

159

The Bikini

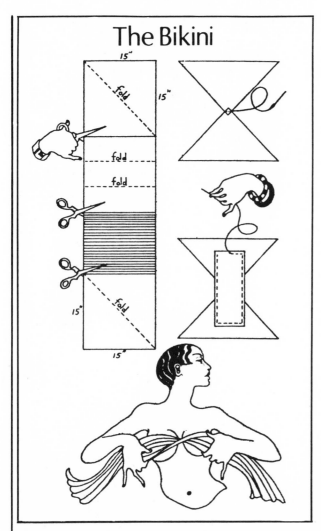

transform the mood of the grimmest institutional room—suddenly it looks personal and creative. You can do the same thing at home for a quick change of mood.

Inventive European models with little money soon develop a knack for finding bits and pieces to make into little, wrapped creations to express their very personal esthetic sense. Christiana Steidten always carries scarves to wrap into a strapless dress, a little bandeau top, or a floaty skirt, as you can see in the photographs.

There are endless ways of doing yourself up in fabric. To start, you might buy a three-yard length of light Indian cotton gauze, the best size for beginners. Take a look at the pictures in this section and start right in, twisting, tying, and tucking. One of the easiest skirts to create is copied from the Balinese. A three-yard length is wrapped

It's silly that the tiniest bikinis fetch ridiculous prices when it is so simple to create your own. It's just a twist of a wrist and two scarves. The ones shown here are 58 by 15 inches. For the bottom, cut the scarf on the solid line and fold on the dotted lines to make the back and front triangles. Fold the remaining material in thirds to make a long rectangle which is stitched in as the crotch; tie the corners at the hips and you have bikini pants. For the top use a similar scarf, same size, twist it in the center and tie snugly in back or at the neck.

What do you do when the occasion calls for a dress and all you've got is jeans? Christiana, like most models, doesn't even bother with dresses. But she has developed the secrets of wrapping. With three yards of fabric, she envelopes her body as if draping a column. She ties a little knot at the top, turns the fabric down like a narrow cuff and accents this simplicity with extra-special accessories.

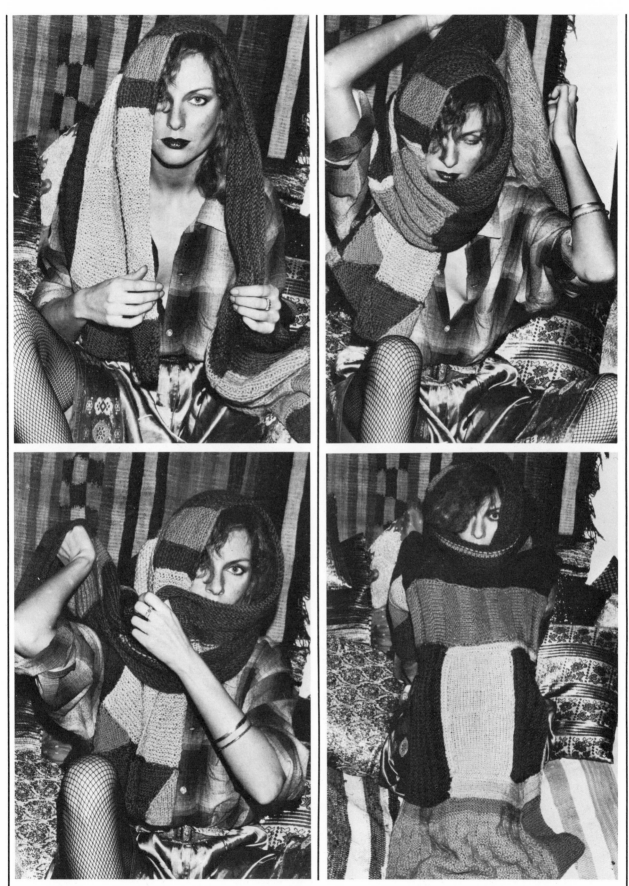

A winter wrap for the snow-bound! Between takes, Christiana calmly knits and what started as a scarf has grown to a wonderful wrapping-blanket, covered with bizarre patterns and combinations of colors. As you can see, even twisting it over her head and neck again and again, she still has enough left over to warm her long legs.

Once in a while you may find yourself near water, wanting to swim but lacking a bathing suit. It's wonderful to go naked, but most places are still uptight about nudity outside the bathtub. With wrapping, you can always roll up your dress, pull the back through your legs, tucking the gathered fabric in the belt. Now you're ready to hit the waves!

around the waist or hips, the extra fabric is folded on top of itself in an accordion pleat at the front, then the material around the waist is folded over on itself to hold the skirt in place.

Rayon or nylon fabric is another inexpensive fabric to experiment with. You can cut yourself a sari length and still have lots left when you buy an $11 nylon georgette sari from an Indian import shop.

If you're uncertain with your knotting and tucking, add some insurance—a belt, tight at the waist, a brooch, or a big solid pin. In Bali they don't use buttons—the standard Balinese blouse is just held together in front with two or three safety pins. Most of the people use standard safety pins; the wealthier have more elegant models based on the same theme. You can put a security safety pin at the waist, the shoulder, or the center of the bosom and emerge with the cheapest chic on the beach!

Although it's quite difficult to get around a big city in wrapped clothes, you can still play with fabrics and patterns by wrapping lengths of cloth around your head. In the winter, nothing feels better than a nice tight head-wrapping. During the day, you can use bobbypins to set your hair in tiny pincurls and wrap it tight with a babushka. At night you may emerge with a superfluffy head.

One long scarf looks great knotted at the back of the head with the ends hanging down. Two Russian peasant flowered wool challis scarves look exotic wrapped and twisted over each other so that the patterns and colors contrast. Several scarves look fantastic folded and tied in the middle as a ponytail at the back of a scarfed head. That way you can have your "hair" and set it too.

Don't just stick to your neighborhood Singer Sewing Center. Polyester double-knits won't do. Try to track down the pure cotton and silks that make the best fabrics for wrapping. The range of silks carried at a little cubbyhole of a shop in Los Angeles called Oriental Silks is breathtaking. This listing hints at the wondrous variations of

The Halter

Another multi-purpose piece of cloth to own is this long rectangle of fine cotton or chiffon. For an instant top, put the scarf around your neck, pulling the ends out equally at arms length in front. Cross one over the other to tie in back. Depending on the length of the piece, you may even be able to bring the ends back around to tie in front.

fabric that still exist in the world: silk pongee, Poa Shan pongee, chefoo pongee, ya kiang pongee, pure silk chiffon so light it floats, China silk, Honan silk, spun silk for lingerie, Soo Chow brocade, silk satin, raw silk shantung, palace silk brocade, silk crepe brocade, Kuan Lo Siok crepe brocade, printed silk crepe, printed twill from Shanghai, silk satin tapestry, tinsel-mixed silk satin (said to be the most exquisite silk exported from the mainland), silk marquisette, silk brocade matting, crepe de Chine, Habotai silk, nubbly white silk, silk gauffer, and Po Po silk crepe.

Wrapped in white fox mixed with yards of tulle, Edita Sherman knows how to make that "grand entrance" and liven any party!

ZANDRA RHODES

Pushing Fabric to Extremes

Zandra Rhodes is an English designer whose chic is not cheap to her customers. But to her, and to anyone willing to work and push their imaginations to the utmost, the results can't be anything but individual and rewarding, whether one is designing clothes or just getting dressed for the day.

Zandra has been doodling, snipping, cutting, dyeing, sewing, pleating, and feathering clothes for almost a decade. Yet, today they sell in the hundreds of dollars, but she started with nothing other than her imagination, perseverance, and a totally fresh approach to what can be done with fabrics. Each new Zandra Rhodes collection becomes more personal, startling, and refined. Zandra's clothes are unlike anything you have ever seen or imagined. Solarized lilies, luminous pinks, ripples of silk jersey, an octopus of chiffon, yard upon yard of squiggled labyrinths unfurling to the tune of a mad samba, and now the grand elegance of minuscule pleats on long burgundy silk, and lace-entwined pastel chiffons.

Far from trying to lead the same life as her moneyed customers, Zandra can often be found slaving away in her overcrowded London workroom wearing patched jeans and a silk jersey top over a black turtleneck, or driving around the States in a sleep-in van.

"I come from a very middle-class family near Dover, you know, sort of your average person. Well, I suppose my mother was rather extraordinary; she worked as a fitter in Paris for the couture house of Worth. She met my father, a truck driver, at one of those typically English ballroom dancing contest evenings. She would wear incredible multilayered bright tulle dancing dresses.

"Later, my mother taught at the college where I studied, so I never learned pattern cutting and practical sewing because that was the class she taught! Instead I studied textile design and went on to the Royal College of Art in London, where Mary Quant and a lot of people with new ideas were studying. That was in the pre-Carnaby Street days of London, and when I started taking my textile designs around to be executed, manufacturers kept saying, 'We can never sell these.' So I set up my own print workshop with a friend. And then when boutiques started springing up everywhere, I opened one with another girl, but we fought like crazy because she didn't like my designs. So I thought I better try my luck in America.

"I had to take a crash course in pattern making and then learn how to fit on a stand. I had no idea what the grain in fabric does. I made some terrible mistakes, but at least I had no preconceptions of how a dress was constructed. It was so lovely for that reason . . . bodices falling all over the place! I'm still learning, and it's only been a few years since I've actually sewn pieces of fabric together.

"Now when I show the collections, I stage a spectacular. For the first one I wanted a great Brazilian carnival feeling, mixed with a masked ball. The people who wear my dresses want to stand out in a crowd, not look quiet and secret.

"The more I try to analyze the kind of

clothes I make, the more I find they stand on their own without precedent. People are buying an original—it's what I see that particular year. Those funny dresses I made one year with holes cut in them might not have sold very well when I did them, but

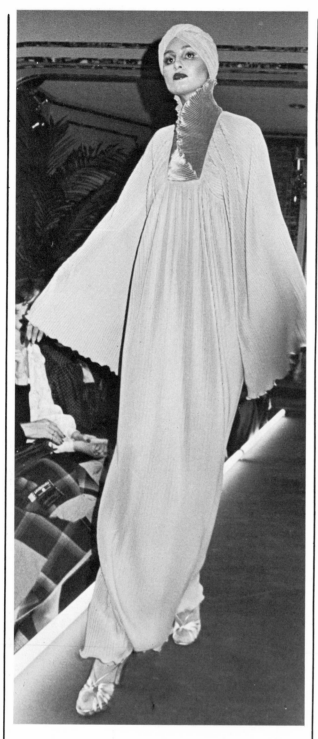

me. My partners used to say, 'For money's sake, Zandra, tone yourself down. You are frightening the buyers away!' But I don't do my makeup to spook people. It just feels fine to me to have fun with colors on my face.

"As long as you are prepared to make mistakes and have other people laugh at you, you can wear and create what you please. I have worn weird things and six months later looked at photographs of myself and thought, 'Oh God, how could I ever have looked like that!' There was one phase where I wore my hair pulled back and painted my face red on the sides. When I look back, it looked terrible, but somehow it was right for me because it pleased me first. I like to pursue ideas that amuse and surprise me, even if they are considered cheap and vulgar by most standards.

"A lot of people I know don't have any money and yet they look very special. It often has to do with the fact that you cannot define the value of what they are wearing, so their personality comes through. Tie a little chiffon handkerchief around your ankle and then wear something completely plain, or add a colored cord for a ring. Why be so status conscious with designer letters all over the place? It's sheer waste. There are plenty of good things everywhere. My bag, which I bought at a London department store five years ago, has gone through everything with me. So what's the point of spending a lot of money on owning a small 'status bag' if I have to carry three paper shopping bags around with it?

"I have to work extra hard because I am always going along my own way. It's not easy; I don't find the act of designing easy at all. I have to shut myself away to do it, even though I like people around. The actual creating part is hell, but the glossy part is easy. When you've done the clothes and you see people galloping around in them, then you're inspired. And you can get back to the locking-yourself-in-the-studio bit. Sometimes I am terrified! My mind becomes a total blank. Actually, I am glad when that happens, because when you get stuck you have to rethink and relook. Then I move along and don't fool myself with the same old ideas."

somewhere along the line they are going to make their mark. I believe my dresses never date. People will wear them ten years from now because I am not involved in trends.

"As far as my own way of getting dressed and made up is concerned, I feel totally immune to what anyone says. That's probably why I sometimes go around with green hair, red cheeks, and iridescent blue dots here and there. It's not that I have a fear of being anonymous. It's something else that drives

WORK CLOTHES

The easiest style for working women is quiet uniformity punctuated with a special personal touch. If we're disillusioned with the high cost of uptown basics, we can track down lovely, inexpensive army-surplus and work clothes. Work clothes were built to fill a need. Since they were never designed to be in fashion, they can never go out of style. And though they are intermittently taken up as fads, whenever a manufacturer tries to knock them off, the imitation comes out looking silly and inept.

Some of the work clothes' colors are a drawback—who wants to look like the school janitor? But if the colors don't match your mood, you can dye them or punctuate them here and there with bright accents. While rejecting fashion, you needn't reject a look of individual charm.

SURPLUS PARADISE

The army-surplus store is the place to head for cheap status. "One might think that status and recession don't marry too well," wrote Enid Nemy in *The New York Times*, "and one might be wrong. The recession is here, but it hasn't driven away status—it's merely reversed it. It's no longer how much one has paid for something, it's how little."

In a time when it's almost impossible to afford top-quality construction, stitching, and fabric, you can find it surplus for low prices. For the person with a tight budget and an aversion to thrift shops, army-surplus stores are a cheap way to dress. The armed services, unlike department stores, do not take delivery on goods that do not meet the strict specifications of their contracts. The stitching is close and tight, the seams are often bound, and buttonholes don't unravel.

Paul vows never to give up his army field jacket.

In a world of synthetic blends and plastic ultrasuede, military clothes are almost the last inexpensive sources of pure cottons, wools, and leathers. And they last *forever*. Army-surplus means never having to say you're sorry.

For those who are still entranced by new silhouettes, perhaps the freshest look is short boots and the bloused pant, dropping to mid-calf or around the ankle, pants a bit big, pulled in at the waist with a knotted belt. This "look" can be seen in Israeli training camps and on the drill fields of Fort Hood, Texas, as well as in fashionable world capitals. It is ironic that a new silhouette is evolving from the regimentation of the military. If you play with these clothes you can develop an individual look. Khaki needn't belong exclusively to the military, just as red isn't the exclusive province of firemen. A regulation army raincoat becomes a nice background when you add a brilliant purple scarf or a fluffy fox collar. The dash of color and the softness of the fur destroy the military character the coat once had.

People were understandably reluctant to go to Vietnam in the sixties, but it seems now that everyone on the street has zipped into the **army field jacket.** For under $10, it's about the cheapest covering around. It's not rainproof, and it isn't too useful without the system designed by the army to go with it—the liner and hood. The field jacket is the hardest popular military design to wear in an individual way. But it does have mystique for some, perhaps it carries the romance of the invisible urban guerrilla.

Fatigues are made of green khaki and once functioned as the army's great equalizer. Within the service an elaborate status system evolved around this basically drab uniform. (Fidel Castro, after all, elevated fatigues to the status of black tie for formal occasions of state.) All military uniforms in America are designed at the U.S. Army's Natick Labs outside Boston. They are meant to work in an ordered system, possible when recruits wear only what they are issued, exactly as issued. But of course, no matter how functional the fatigues were, a soldier had to tighten up on the basic theme, embroider it, embolden it, upset the army's

order—for his personal dignity if nothing else. When recruits cut down and tailored their fatigues for that tight, sexy fit, the Natick "life support system" was shot to hell. The system was based on layering, but there was no way these soldiers could squeeze their winter sweaters and socks under tight fatigues. Luckily, we're not in the army and don't have to go on winter maneuvers or listen to the rules from Natick, so we can get our fatigues in any size, dye them any color, wear them loose or tight, or even chop off the sleeves or legs . . . systems be damned!

The army **fatigue shirt** is like a shirt and jacket rolled into one, with nice big pockets over each breast and sturdy welt seams. You can wear it tight as a glove over a turtleneck, unbuttoned to a knotted waist over a tan, or as a summer jacket with the sleeves rolled up over a T-shirt and drawstring-waisted cotton muslin skirt.

Fatigue pants are designed to be bloused over boots. The army rule is that trousers are not to hang above boot tops, a holdover from World War I leggings which protected against mustard gas on the battlefield.

The aviator's companion, a durable navy blue nylon, fur-collared blouson jacket, which comes with a detachable quilted lining is made all the more attractive by this pilot.

Natick came up with **jungle fatigues** for the war in Vietnam, with roomy, snap pockets on the thigh and bloused drawstring legs that tied mid-calf at the boot to intercept insects and bugs.

It's best to buy fatigues that are older, because the modern "new army" has done away with pure cottons. Starched fatigues used to be a point of pride in the sixties—"breaking starch" meant putting on a nice crisp pair of fashionably faded fatigues—but now the army is designing things for washing machines rather than breaking starch. Fatigues are now of wash-and-wear synthetic blends.

You'll find it's difficult to get both a tight fit in the crotch and enough length in the leg in almost any military uniform, so consider taking them to a seamstress. Tuck the short pants into high boots or under a pair of crazy socks. (Take a look at the chapter on sports clothes: hockey socks? Baseball gaiters? Soccer stripes, perhaps?)

Several schools of blousing developed in the army over the years, and you might as well know what they are.

1. The George Washington School. The pant's leg is folded around the ankle, wrapped with 3-M® masking tape to hold the fabric tight, and then inserted into the boot.

2. The Blousing Rubber School. The blousing rubber is a big green fabric-covered elastic band similar to a ponytail holder. The band is snapped around the ankle, the trouser leg is tucked up under the inside of the rubber band, and *voilá*, a simple blouse.

3. The Blousing Ring School. The one person in ten who seeks true perfection inserts a heavy metal blousing ring, about six inches in diameter, down the leg of the trousers before using the blousing rubbers. The weight of the metal ring gives the bottom of the blouse that perfect, rounded shape. In theory, the blousing ring refinement is rather like the tiny golden chains Coco Chanel placed in the lining of her suit jackets to make them hang perfectly.

4. The Tin Can School. A number-ten vegetable can with both ends cut out and

taped is slid down the pants leg to give a smooth, even, blouse above the boots, but tends to clank while walking. Some blousing experts prefer a *Time* or *Newsweek*-sized magazine slipped inside the pants to give a stiff look to the leg. A magazine is much quieter than a tin can, and you can read it if you get stuck in line!

Once you've mastered the arcane art of blousing, you might as well top it all off with an olive drab cotton cap. Don't go too all-out with fatigues, or men will turn from you with horrible memories of mosquito-spattered training at Parris Island. Tuck in a blue pack of Gauloise cigarettes in the waist, put a pumpkin-bright T-shirt under the top, tie on a long, multicolored silk jersey scarf, turn up the collar and sleeves,

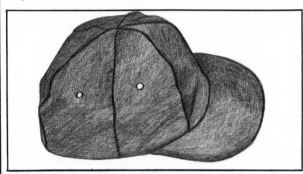

blouse the pants into your favorite boots, and you're Cheap Chic. The surplus outfit basics shouldn't cost more than $13–$15.

If you're one of those purists who search high and low for **pure wool socks,** we have it on good authority that the army issues the finest socks of the world's finest wool. Of course, they come in olive drab, but you can't have everything! At Brooks Brothers they would cost $5. Some surplus stores carry the British army sweater of thick-ribbed wool with canvas shoulder patches.

The **army-issue undershirt** is made of wool and cotton with a big crew neck and a long, long, knitted cuff on the sleeves. In a big size on a thin girl, it looks like a drop-shouldered beach dress, especially when tied up with a brass-buckled web belt or a classic silver antique or conch belt. Also nice in summer is the $1 khaki cotton undershirt. The quality is much better than comparably priced discount-store undershirts.

What a way to go to work—practical, loose and protected.

The big, mid-calf **army raincoat** is a fashionable alternative to getting wet. Over a sweater or two, it can function as a year-round raincoat. The designers of this coat weren't stingy: there is lots of room here for layering, because the cut is really ample. Not bad for $6.

A pilot's one-piece **flight suit** looks like a dashing coverall, with a zipped front and two diagonally cut zip pockets on the chest, and pockets here and there for maps and things. They come in brown or olive, cotton

175

or wool, and at $15–$20 could be a year-round uniform over a silk shirt or turtle-neck, or under a leather vest. (But remember that the jumpsuit and coveralls were designed for men. Like the leotard, it can be difficult to unlayer yourself when you have to run to the bathroom.) If you grow inordinately fond of the airman look, sink some money into a weathered leather flight jacket lined and collared with fluffy wool shearling. This jacket develops a rich and romantic patina with age and proper care.

For a more conservative effect, look for the below-the-knees classic blue wool **air force officer's overcoat.** They really knew how to make these right, and if you set a tailor to work on it, you can wear this coat from Wall Street to Walden Pond with ease. In quality and design, the officers coat is equal to a made-to-measure overcoat.

The dark blue **navy pea coat** is another almost-luxurious military classic, beauti-

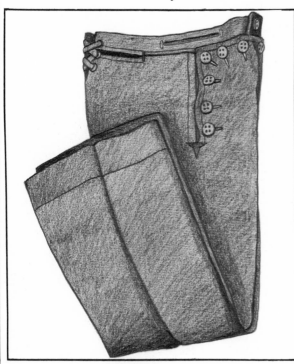

Pants that take forever to unbutton but last and last.

fully designed in quality wool. Yves St. Laurent copied it almost line for line in his couture collection a few years ago and is returning to it again. You can get the original design for much less at your local army-navy store.

The navy blue **thirteen-button wool sailor pants** with black lacings can take you

A navy captain's coat is fine protection against winter wind.

through many winters, but beware of length because they are often too short to wear with heels.

The U. S. Navy also makes the very best **100 percent wool sweater** in a flat dark-blue knit that will keep you toasty warm and good looking. The navy sweater comes with long or three-quarter length sleeves for under $10. To keep your head warm, pull an inexpensive knitted navy watch cap down over your ears. (Your hair gets brittle, and over half your body heat can be lost by an uncovered head in the bitter cold, so cover it! Ears too.)

Navy surplus is also a rich source for perfect pale blue cotton **workshirts.** Sak's, Bloomingdale's, I. Magnin's, and Macy's all

WORK CLOTHES

American work clothes have been around in one form or another since the country was built, working on the railroad, down in the coal mines, busting sod, putting up skyscrapers, and digging subways. Their functional style evolved from a long line of anonymous designers and the demands of hard work. They've got integrity, stamina, good looks, and oh you kid!

Coveralls are worn by mechanics, freaks, artists, and just plain folks. Antonio Lopez, one of the most original fashion illustrators of New York and Paris, wears $20 khaki coveralls every day: "They're so comfortable and made so well that I live in them!" It is intriguing to think that Antonio—who

sell dippy imitations in polyester-and-cotton blends, but the navy makes the real McCoy. Starched and pressed and teamed up with a fine silk tie, some men wear them daily to the office to give a tongue-in-cheek note to the suit-and-tie tradition.

More high style that can sometimes be discovered at army-surplus stores: Beige twill **shorts** with buttoned cartridge pockets and epaulets; khaki cotton pleated **walking shorts;** the classic **safari jacket** with epaulets, breast and hip pockets, back pleat and belt. The safari jacket is another military classic that has made its way from the streets to the couture houses of Paris. It's $80 at Abercrombie & Fitch, under $15 at a surplus store. Take a look in First Layers (Chapter I) to see how one woman uses the safari jacket as the year-round top-layer in a flexible clothing system. The U. S. Army Natick clothing labs would be ever so proud.

Work or no work, the real safari jacket, above left, is a traveler's most useful carry-all-in-the-pockets piece of clothing, though the look can get lumpy. For heavy-duty activity, gloves are a must with the basic coverall. John Wayne took advantage of their charm a long time ago. Hurray for the hard-hats.

180 | **Rediscovered in the seventies: The classic French jeweler's smock has remained unchanged for centuries.**

discovers and styles some of the most beautiful and eccentric fashion models in the world—is fond of going around town in the lowly coverall.

Can't Bust 'Em brand coveralls have a multitude of pockets and are meant to withstand grease and grime and heavy washing, so a little city dirt doesn't faze them. Sweet Orr overalls in brown hard-hat style make you feel like a construction worker, with their bib front and suspender back. In gray pinstripes, they make you want to ride the rails; in denim you can tame the West or wrassle a commune to its knees.

What's blue, denim, and very baggy? **Carpenters' pants,** with a fascinating array of pockets down the side and mysterious loops and fasteners for hammers, chisels, rules, and flat pencils. Find them in white and dye them any shade you like. **Painters' pants** are another cheap, stylish way to dress.

Checked wool **lumberjack shirts** from

army-surplus stores are a handsome, sturdy classic, and the more expensive Pendleton soft wool plaid shirts are a worthwhile investment. Wear one under a riding jacket with a butterfly bow tie.

European work clothes offer all the good design and construction of the American breed, and give you that extra ripple of pleasure from finding something cheap, stylish, and really unique that no one has yet. Looking for work clothes is one way to see more of what a country's all about. A

Janitor's wear, the beige twill shirt, gets all dolled up.

friend of ours brought back a pair of pinstriped gray overalls from Prague just after the Russians had occupied Czechoslovakia. The saleswoman couldn't understand a country where rich students preferred wearing work clothes, and our friend couldn't understand why the Czechs didn't see the inherent beauty of a well-designed pair of overalls. It was an international standoff, but the Czech overalls were a big hit back in Boston.

La Samaritaine, the biggest department store in Paris, has several floors full of some very unexpected, beautiful work clothes. Their oatmeal linen **jewelers' smock** makes a very chic dress, with ample fabric gathered from an overstitched neckband and loose, gusseted sleeves. La Samaritaine also carries well-tailored overalls, black coal-man's suits, ciré fishmongers' tops, nuns' aprons, painters' smocks, dress-length sculptors' smocks, blue cotton electricians' jackets, butchers' smocks, and medical uniforms; all unchanged for a hundred years.

Cheap protection against the rain is a simple beret along with a basic private's raincoat found at the surplus stores.

La Blouse des Halles is another Paris work-clothes headquarters. Here you can find bright orange polyester zip-up coveralls, a butchers' jacket in a small hound's-tooth check, the white garçon de café waiters' jacket in prices ranging from $15 to $20. The long doctors' coats are cool and crisp for summer, and cheap at $13; or you can fashion your own white "linen" suit by getting a $9 medical jacket to wear with sailor pants and a bright scarf.

The shop Sotovol in Paris caters to race-car drivers and aviators. The special Numero Uno **jumpsuit** opens with dual zippers from neck to leg, so you can put it on over everything you're wearing. This design has a stand-up officer's collar, chest and hip pockets, and two map pockets on the side of the leg. All this intricacy costs $50. It comes ready to wear or made to measure in poplin or gabardine of slate blue, mouse gray, chestnut brown, taupe, beige, or white. Or choose the parachutist's camouflage piebald coverall for $32.

There is also an extremely stylish shop in Paris called Globe, so severe it looks like a

Take this white cotton jacket out of context, and you have comfortable, chic summer wear.

locker room. The owner sees work clothes as the only logical way to dress after the thirties-to-sixties revivals with all their kitsch overtones. In the midst of these riotous shapes and colors, Globe leans toward a sober chic which can look rather somber. If you wish to pass quiet and unnoticed, Globe will outfit you with work clothes imported from all over the world: French, English, and American army/navy uniforms from around the world, Chinese padded jackets, and Japanese street-workers' pants

By gosh, Osgood never tires of his Osh-Kosh.

A uniform, dyed a favorite color, could be a favorite dress.

and kimonos. "You say khaki looks sad," says the owner, Gerard Decoster, "but is shocking pink as gay as all that? I've been wearing khaki for six years now, and I've had a ball every day. And besides, for the quality of cut, stitch, and fabric, you can't find a better bargain."

PROFESSIONAL UNIFORMS

A Japanese painter lives in New York, buys medical uniforms, dyes them, and sells them to expensive department stores. She uses a particularly Japanese palette which ranges from dusky roses to deep violets that take beautifully on white cottons. Her most popular uniforms are the short surgical gowns and long wraparound patients' gowns with loose raglan sleeves and little ties in the front, short wraparound operating jackets, button-front cotton short-sleeved nurses' uniforms, and three-quarter-length duck lab coats. Other specialties are hand-dyed 50¢ cotton petticoats with eyelet-trimmed

hems found on Fourteenth Street and sold for summers at the beach with an undershirt of a similar shade.

Hotel and restaurant supply houses carry perfect white waiters' jackets, kitchen pants, and big wraparound aprons to color for summer covering and winter jumper

183

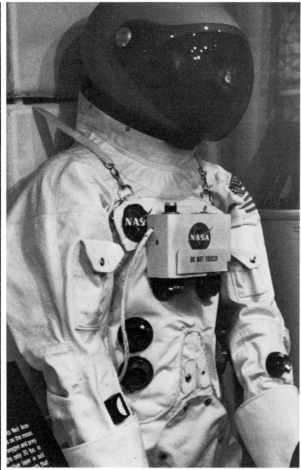

The most perfect and advanced of all jumpsuits or work clothes is also the most useless garment for earth-wear!

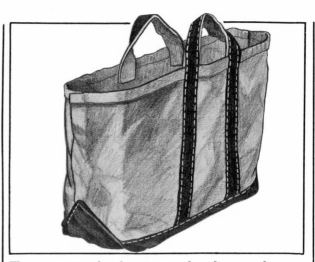

The canvas tote for shopping, week-ending, or whatever.

wear. You can find large **canvas totes** at supply houses such as the All-Steel Scale Company in New York. They sell mail totes and leather-trimmed canvas bank-note bags that you can have monogramed and made to order in the size you like for $30 to $50.

If you're looking for an inexpensive yet classic blazer, track down the department store that carries uniforms for the most exclusive girls' or boys' school in town. One friend of ours in San Francisco bought a single-breasted navy wool school blazer which was actually the uniform for Miss Burke's School, added special English buttons, had it shaped by a seamstress, and has been wearing it on and off since 1962. It now needs only a new lining—not bad for $30. While you're in the uniform department, see if you can dig up a crisp little nanny's dress, a school's cotton shirtwaist, or sturdy brown walking shoes. School clothes are rather appealing once you're not forced to wear them. The best places to find

used school blazers are the exchanges run by the private schools to raise money for charity and scholarships. The Spence-Chapin Exchange in New York occasionally has uniforms on its racks, and once in a while an absolutely breathtaking couture debutante gown will make an appearance.

If you have a little girl, ask friends going to France to buy the adorable little button-front, long-sleeved school uniform called a "tablier," which can be found in most hosiery or haberdashery shops for $1. The older the store, the bigger the chance of finding an old stock of these pure cotton uniforms.

Wendy frolicks in her "le tablier" school-girl dress.

184

Fanciful Young American Design

Dear friends — I'M HAPPY TO HAVE THE CHANCE TO WRITE TO YOU......to LET YOU KNOW HOW MUCH I APPRECIATE YOUR INTEREST IN MY WORK. I ESPECIALLY ENJOY HEARING FROM SOME OF YOU...FRIENDLY LITTLE LETTERS, LETTING ME KNOW THAT YOU'VE MADE UP ONE OF MY PATTERNS + YOU LIKE IT A LOT....MAKES ME FEEL VERY GOOD. ...KEEPS ME GOING. SO I THOUGHT I'D LIKE YOU TO KNOW ME BETTER.

Betsey Johnson sizzled onto the fashion scene in 1965 as top designer for Paraphernalia, where she kept churning out unique styles—the skinny T-shirt dress, tiny undershirt tops, miniskirted A-lines—pop clothes that were a jumping reflection of those heady days of the "youth revolution." Betsey was our own homegrown Mary Quant, a designer of immense talent and energy. She went on to Puritan, Alvin Duskin, Alley Cat, Capezio, I. Miller Shoes, and is now starting afresh in several fields: basic T-shirt dressing for Tric-Trac, designer patterns for Butterick, and collections of sweaters, shirts, maternity clothes, and children's things for Penney's (Betsey just had her first baby). She's signed on for only two seasons with everyone, "to get myself in a position of strength." She continues her involvement

SUN + MOON IN LEO...TAURUS RISING.

ME. AUGUST 10, 1942. WETHERSFIELD, CONN. THE ONLY THING I KNEW WAS THAT NOBODY COULD GET ME OUT OF MY HAND-ME-DOWN LITTLE RED WOOL DRESS.. WITH REAL PEARL BUTTONS!? MAYBE MA MADE IT. WHEN I HAVE KIDS I'M GOING TO MAKE THEM EVERYTHING THEY PUT ON.

MAYBE CHILDREN'S PATTERNS...NEXT. TOY CLOTHES!

with Betsey, Bunky, and Nini, a New York boutique that serves as a laboratory of ideas for Betsey.

"All my work is really a good time. I approach it thinking 'would I want to wear it?' But I don't want the manufacturers to think the way that I look is the way my work looks. I want to get them to think of my work as separate. So I wear my housedresses or old jerseys up to their offices. After leaving Alley Cat I realized that I had this terrible freaky Junior Designer image, and it's hard negotiating with businessmen who are trying to play dumb and pretend that they think you can't design anything else. But all these stupid jobs become challenges to do what I wanted! Like with the sweaters. It's a challenge to use cut chenilles and mohairs and the colors I want. Despite the problems, I love mass-

185

market and inexpensive stretchy stuff. I'm from the wrong side of the tracks to be doing a custom social thing. I like to work in a very isolated way—a private clientele would involve a lot of socializing.

"My ideas come from everywhere—I guess you'd say I'm eclectic. I get ideas from the costumes I used to make for dancing school as a kid; from those T-shirty kinds of baby clothes. I go to the textile library at the Metropoiltan Museum—but if they see you doing anything more than looking, they rush out with big sheets of plastic to protect the fabric! And I visit the Philadelphia Museum, which has a great collection of old American work clothes. In terms of countries, I get most ideas from South America, India, and Turkey. I used to make fabrics and clothes out of India, Turkey, and Hong Kong. And colors—in Burma, those saffron-robed monks in the middle of all those shades of green—that registers later, when you're designing. I rip off old peasant clothes, but I put my own touch in there always!

"I'm so tactile that when I teach for free I blindfold the kids so they can really feel things. I think that the tactile sense is the most important thing to have in your work, being able to feel how something is going to fit on your body.

"My ideal would be to sell one item a week on a corner, Saturday afternoons. The people would know I'd be on the corner with pants one week, then matching tops the next . . . that way I could do what I wanted in any colors that I wanted, and they wouldn't be marked up. I know women I'd love to have here in my loft just sewing, sewing. If you keep it to one style a week a lady can make it quite fast. Of course, you'd have to guess at the fit. You couldn't try my things on, just like Biba T-shirts. But I think the person I sell things to has a sense of holding things up to her body and seeing if they fit. I never try things on when I shop. But that's my dream—a street-corner operation—because I never have an outlet to do exactly what I want. I know I'm more proud of the T-shirts and pants and drawstring skirts than of all the expensive, overdone things at Betsey, Bunky, and Nini, where I know the prices are too high but don't have any control!"

186

MAYBE CHILDREN'S PATTERNS . . . NEXT . TOY CLOTHES? MAYBE

OH . . . I REALLY WANTED TO BE A DANCER . . . . . MY GREAT TEACHER WOULD LET ME DESIGN ALL MY SOLO COSTUMES. MY MOTHER MADE THEM . I STILL HAVE EVERY ONE. I'D MAKE DOLL CLOTHES OUT OF THE VERY UNUSUAL FABRICS, SEQUINS, CHINA SILK, TARLETAN, LAMÉ + GLITTERED NETTING.

TOO BAD . . . NOTHING AS FANTASTIC AS PARAPHERNALIA COULD LAST.

+ HERE'S ME IN A TV STUDIO IN NEW YORK . . . THE ALL TIME "CITY OF MY DREAMS". AFTER GETTING AN ART DEGREE, WINNING MLLE. G.E. CONTEST . . . WORKIN' AT MLLE MAG . . . GOT A JOB AT THE MOST FANTASTIC "DESIGN WORKSHOP" (1965) . . . . . I COULD ALWAYS SEW + MAKE MY OWN PATTERNS . . . + FOR 3 YEARS MADE ANYTHING I WANTED TO . . . . I LIVED IN SILVER TAP SHOES, TEENY TINY SKIRTS + REALLY STARTED DOING MY BODY-BASIC T-SHIRT STUFF.

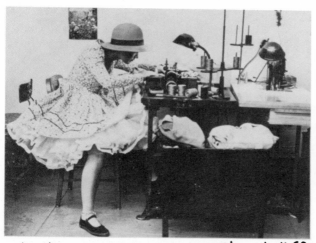

INDIA WHERE I LIKE TO GO MOST.

OH DEAR.... MY "BRAID-OFF THE BOAT PERIOD"- (JUST OVER.) I'M A LITTLE SWEDISH + LIKE TO WEAR PEASANT CLOTHES BEST. THE EARLY 70'S- I WAS DOING MY "OWN THING" NOT WANTING TO LOOK LIKE ANYONE OR ANYTHING.

SO... HAPPILY ON TO "ALLEY CAT" + BUTTERICK... A.C'S GROWING UP.. BUT BUTTERICK IS GETTING MORE + MORE FUN. LOTS OF "CRAFTY" STUFF... LIKE THE IRON-ON DRAWINGS "APRON-KIT". I LOVE TO MAKE THINGS THAT NO MANUFACTURER COULD TURN OUT IN MASS-PRODUCTION. VERY PERSONAL... CREATIVE THINGS MADE WITH CARE + PRIDE. FOR BUTTERICL I'M GOING TO STICK WITH "CRAFT" THINGS...

GODFREY... I LOVE CLUTTER! HERE'S MY WORKROOM... I LIKE CLOTHES TO LOOK LIKE THIS. VERY PERSONAL, LOTS TO LOOK AT. EVERYTHINGS AN IDEA OR SOMETHING THAT AMUSES ME... OR JUNK.

I THINK ITS BEST TO SAY HERE.... THAT YOU CAN DO ANYTHING YOU REALLY WANT TO.... THERE'S NO "SECRET" WAY. JUST LOVE + DESIRE... I THINK.... + AS A FRIEND JUST TOLD ME... REMEMBER.... YOU CAN NEVER HAVE TOO MUCH FUN......

+ YES... MY DEAR WORKROOM "LADIES" THAT MAKE MY DAYS PEACEFUL + HAPPY. WE'VE ALL BEEN TOGETHER FOR YEARS. CHELENA, EMMA, MAGDA + CHERRY ALL WORKING TOGETHER... OUR FAMILY. APART FROM THE "RAG" BUSINESS.

+ TODAY.... HENNA IN MY HAIR ... STILL BASICALLY IN T-SHIRTS + FUNNY BOTTOMS. I'M MOVING INTO A BIG LOFT DOWNTOWN + FEEL LIKE I'M STARTING FRESH. THAT FEELS GOOD. XOXO LOVE, BETSEY.

JOHN LOMBARDI

A Raffish
Mix for the Tieless Office

John Lombardi has worked for Rolling Stone *in San Francisco,* Oui *in Chicago, and* Esquire *in New York. He now lives in New York and writes with great wit and perception. He is almost always the most individual - looking man in the office without ever losing his basic sense of humorous elegance.*

"When I was twenty I wore a motorcycle jacket and boots on a campus where the students were mostly dressed in preppy tweeds and button-downs. I wanted to stand out, and I did. I also became almost another person and acted like I thought he would act. Still later, when everyone had begun to use clothes in the way I was using them, I started customizing whatever trendy looks were around. I mixed up my daydreams, and so I developed my own style: like wearing a jean shirt and flared Levi's, faded to the same color, worn with antique orange cowboy boots and a genuine floppy old-time velvet bow tie. This made me a cowboy with a touch of elegance and a touch of hipness. Or I'd wear a St. Laurent suit over a motley purple T-shirt that I got used for fifty cents, with black-and-white custom-made specta-tor shoes from England. I was laughing at fashion because I knew I could never dress like a model in a magazine but could look okay my way.

"Mixing things is the key to the way I dress. Mixing seems current and it lets me use my dreams, which come from all over the place and keep changing. It's also cheaper.

"I got a fur coat for $50 in a flea market in Paris. It's some kind of monkey fur. I've had it for four years, and I'll have it for the rest of my life, because it brings Paris back in a flash, and I liked myself in Paris.

"These leather pants were made for me. They cost $135, but again, I'll have them for a long time, unless I get fat! They're made of deerskin and look fine with velvet or leather jackets, sweaters and T-shirts. They also look okay with sandals, sneakers, and beat-up or dressy boots. Depending on what I wear these pants with, I can feel like a male hustler, a modern cowboy, a French director, or a member of the wedding.

"I don't think clothes should take up too much time. You should indulge yourself a little, like daydreaming, and then you should forget about what you look like."

THE MIXES

Once you have set up your basic uniform, a few special classics, and some thrift-shop finds, how do you go about putting them together for the way you live, be it in Portland, Oregon; Albuquerque, New Mexico, or Buffalo, New York? This chapter will show you the different ways people put themselves together. They can be quite extreme, but we think you will find hints, ideas, and inspirations from all of them. We want you to see the kinds of individual styles that never make it to the fashion magazines. Ultimately, the crux of Cheap Chic is learning to put things together for the person you imagine yourself to be. Some of you may want exotic evening fantasies; others may go for a sexy but ladylike elegance; and others, just that special accessory that lifts the basics out of the uniform category and gives you an individual stamp. The way you put things together tells others and yourself that you care about feeling good, which is, after all, the point of

A pair of over-the-knee socks give jeans the look of short-shorts; a wrapped waist makes the shirt a jacket.

variety of styles to play with and very few salesladies to guide us down Chic Street. All we have to go on is our eye, our sense of adventure, and (hopefully) the spirit to look as great as possible. We can occasionally make real idiots out of ourselves when we go to extremes, but as the eccentric English designer Zandra Rhodes says, "It's not the fact that one is always right, but if you say something is attractive with enough conviction, people are going to believe you, even if it's wrong!" Without a bit of experimentation, a bit of disaster even, it is difficult to develop that strong sense of personal style that doesn't cost any more than a basic uniform but yields a sense of personal artistry. So plunge in and don't be afraid to make a "mistake."

A crepe-de-Chine scarf tied and twisted looks like two.

looking good. Clothes let you live out your visual fantasies and please others in the process.

Back in the fifties, putting yourself together used to be called "mix and match." There were relatively simple, boring rules for creating an ensemble: the bag matched the shoes, which matched the gloves and hat; all, of course, color coordinated to the stiff two-piece suit, matching blouse, and belt. Even lipstick and nail polish got into the mix-and-match act. Five-and-dime heiress Barbara Hutton, it was said, used to change her nail polish three times a day to match the different-colored dresses she wore. Thank heavens we're out from under that oppressive fashion yoke! Today we have total, exciting, exhilarating freedom to wear absolutely anything. We have an endless

THE ITALIAN MIX

Daniela Morera is an Italian woman with a throaty, Lauren Bacall voice, and a strong style to match. The strength of her looks comes from the imagination she spends, not the money. Her clothes are a crazy mix of antiques handed down from her grandmother, purchases from army-surplus stores, men's classic tailoring, and beautiful ethnic acces-

At night, Daniela Morera flaunts her Dark Lady look: transparent, embroidered tulle, sometimes with "birds wings" over the breasts, sometimes not, depending on the social climate. She made the "Schiaparelli" hat from an Indian import, found the fur at a used clothing shop.

sories. Daniela will, for instance, mix cheap green paratrooper pants with a pair of good boots, a silk blouse, and a boy's unlined corduroy jacket; in other words, classics and work clothes. But then she'll add the little twists that really march this outfit right out of the ordinary:

• A crepe de Chine square tied around the back of the head peasant style, then knotted and twisted and looped around the front of her head and tied. The geometric and paisley grounds in the scarf make it look as if she's layered two pieces of fabric, and the knotting gives a strong profile.
• A cheap black Lucite-and-horn walking stick from Haiti
• Fingerless, brightly patterned Peruvian knit gloves
• A self-assured stance and slim body to carry it all off.

If you can't insinuate yourself into a look like this, it just won't work. Try on a tough look for size. It's all done with mixing things from the main chapters of this book and adding some special accessories. Wear the look several times, and if you still feel uncomfortable, pass on to something new.

Experiment constantly until you find just what you feel good in and just what the local traffic will bear.

Ethnic clothes can be so adaptable to Western looks that they become beautifully invisible. A classic $30 beige Balinese cotton blouse appliquéd with pale violets becomes a simply lovely evening outfit when put together with a double-layered silk

The Milano Mix is a dash of Army surplus, a bit of Belotti silk, seasoned well with men's tailoring and dry humor.

georgette skirt. Daniela found the fabric where she works and had the skirt made up by her Italian seamstress. The outfit at this point is nice for evening, but not exceptional. What Daniela has done to take it that one step further is to add her own stamp—"bird's wings" and "non-jewel jewelry."

• "Bird's wings" are several beautiful feathers glued together in a small, curved wing and attached to each breast with double-faced Scotch tape. Daniela wanted to know "how to be sexy, but not vulgar, especially in Europe, where the clubs and restaurants are more conservative." So many evening dresses these days are cut low in front, or fashioned of light fabric, or slit to the waist, that it is impossible to wear a bra. The feathers are her solution for almost-transparent clothes.

• Non-jewel jewelry skirts the issues of real versus fake by going in another direction entirely: Daniela makes up her "jewelry" by exploring trimmings shops and notions departments and making her own decorations, in this case a feathered and knotted, violet-velvet rope.

The result of these two individual touches is a highly stylized aura—all created with a lot of experimentation, a willingness to make mistakes, and very little money.

Daniela's dark-lady look for sophisticated evenings is all built around a piece of embroidered tulle her grandmother gave her, plus:

• The hot-pink pillbox she perches above her eyebrows, actually an embroidered Indian cap she has had for ages. One day, she figured if she put a center crease in it, the hat would acquire a provocative air. She folded it like a World War II GI cap, set it on the floor, and balanced about twenty phone books on top. It sat, and sat, and sat, until after seven days and seven nights an original emerged.

• The seamed, sparkled stockings are the finishing touch for the dark-lady look. Daniela always hunts down antique hose. Sometimes she even finds the old rayon-seamed stockings that were the only pre-war, pre-nylon alternative to silk. She uses

Elmer's Glue-All to add colored rhinestones to either side of the seam, and then accentuates her legs with the highest, most stiletto-heeled, sexiest shoes she can find.

LINGERIE

Those night-sparkled seamed stockings give us a hint as to what lingerie has become in recent years, more an accessory than a necessity. It wasn't until the early seventies that the full range of underwear stopped selling: the half-slips, full-slips, panties, bras, girdles,

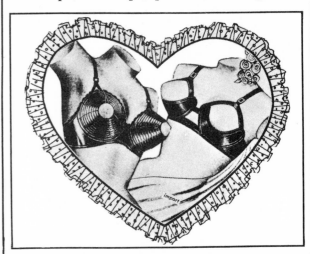

The bra: Frederick's of Hollywood thinks less is more.

or garter belts with thigh-high stockings. Once these items went out of favor, brains started to percolate, and stylish girls realized that these once-utilitarian items can be put to the nonutilitarian uses of enticement, seduction, and humor. Seamed stockings with a garter belt are downright sexy, especially with a pair of marabou-trimmed satin mules. You can even pull off the effect of seamed stockings when wearing pantyhose. Biba makes seamed pantyhose in a mind-boggling array of colors for under $1 a pair. If a friend goes to London, ask her to buy some for you in the one-size-fits-all.

Tight panties and bikinis can be rotated with silky, open-leg, lace-trimmed shorts, like the ones worn in the twenties. These floppy pants allow the body to breathe, and look surprisingly sexy, both naive and knowing. Fernando Sanchez designs the sensuous underwear that shows up in the fashion magazines and is being copied by

Fishnet stockings and high heels have been a sexy come-on since the days of the Gold Rush.

all the manufacturers, but thrift shops still hide the most luscious pure-silk styles. Even if your underpinnings never show, you get a charge of erotic energy just knowing you're wearing the most beautiful, silkiest lingerie imaginable under your plain T-shirt and jeans. Or, on the other hand, you may get the same effect knowing you are wearing the tackiest, hardest sex-queen lingerie ordered directly from the catalog master himself, Mr. Frederick of Hollywood.

NAUGHTY BUT NICE

Holly Harp has probably never worn a Mr. Frederick's original, but she doesn't have to. Her designs have been described by customers as "naughty but nice," just the kind of thing for the sexy, body-conscious, but upstanding ladies of Los Angeles. Clothes that bear her label are expensive, but

Holly's sensuous jerseys: the dirndyl pants are a day and night constant. Here, a silk crepe de Chine head-wrap, antique fur, and her dyed jersey bandeau.

Holly's style doesn't have to cost a lot. It's a system of simple, sometimes whimsical, clothes centered around her basic silk jersey dirndl pants and, quite often, her exercise leotard. The mix will take her from her factory to exercise class to a party in the Hollywood Hills. Because of the free and open way people dress in southern California, Holly never worries about looking overdressed. She just wears what pleases her.

The Holly touches that enliven her basics are:

• A scalloped capelet that was a *Ladies' Home Journal* home sewing project in the forties, decorated with mysterious drippings she has not been able to re-create.
• A piece of chiffon made into a belt for the twenties diamenté belt buckle she found at a thrift shop.
• A silk crepe de Chine scarf wrapped around her head, peasant-style.

All her colors are in a muted range of smoky violets, grays, and greens, so everything mixes with everything else. The strong, simple impact of Holly's style leaves little room for showy jewels or accessories. Cheap Chic comes in knowing when to subtract from a look as well as when to add to it.

These pants are Holly's "jeans." Here she wears them with an old belt, capelet, and Lycra exercise leotard.

SHORT CUTS

Wearing a pair of **shorts** in town is even trickier than looking good in a bikini on the beach. You may be able to kid yourself about the shape of your upper thighs, but is anyone else going to go along with the joke? If your thighs are sizable, do some spot exercises and stay away from shorts. But if you do have marvelous legs, celebrate the fact with some wonderfully floppy shorts, wide at the top of the leg and very, very short. Shorts are a form of feminine brinksmanship. Sporting-goods stores are full of bright shorts if you want to play this game.

Knit **socks** may sound rather dowdy, but

Think of buying shorts in multiples once you find a pair that curves where you curve.

an enterprising use of long and short socks is another secret way of giving yourself a new look, a new proportion, and a sexier kind of walk, all with the same old clothes. For instance, you can pull a pair of above-the-knee hockey socks up under short, floppy shorts, and slip on a pair of beautiful red leather Tibetan boots with little turned-up toes.

Or try long woolly underwear socks pulled thigh high over tightly pegged jeans, leaving just a strip of denim thigh. Or go one step further by layering a shorter pair of striped basketball socks over the woolies. For very chilly weather, thick, natural-wool socks look fantastic with peasant clogs and rolled-up jeans, coveralls, or a big, quilted

Don't rely on Lady Luck; ask to see a tattooist's work.

top. If you roll down another thick pair of knee socks to make a fat cuff around the ankle, you have made a completely new look out of a couple of pairs of socks and some imagination.

Think of socks as a cheap way of changing your whole look rather than a mere covering for the feet. The same goes for **thermal underwear,** which can become an overblouse, vest, or dress. Thermal underwear looks especially Rabelaisian teamed with fat old suspenders, or, as they say in Britain, braces.

SELF-ADORNMENT

The final, irreversible decorative effect you can make is the **tattoo,** a form of permanent jewelry, an intriguing holdover from primitive man's attempt at personal adornment. A tattoo tells the world you're going for broke. If you are intrigued by the idea, be sure to

A tattoo with an Eastern touch and mystical properties.

choose a design (or "flash," as they're called in the trade) that will not go out of style in five years. And don't be taken in by the tattoos on the body of the prospective tattooist. That is not his work. Some of the

Facial tattoos are cheap, but permanent, adornment.

sloppiest tattoo artists have some of the most beautiful tattoos on their bodies. Check out the artist's work carefully. Or wait until you can take a trip to Japan, where the tattoos are the most beautiful and classic of all. If your skin is to become a work of art, it should dazzle forever, not become a shabby reminder of misplaced enthusiasm.

Having **pierced ears** is less permanent than a tattoo but seems to require almost the same amount of daring. Maybe the idea of pierced flesh still holds some atavistic thrill for us. If you change your mind later, the hole will grow over, leaving just a tiny scar. And pierced ears are actually sensible: earrings are easier to wear with pierced ears because they can't squeeze and pinch the ear lobe like snap-back ear clips. Should you go on to have two, three, four, or more holes pierced in each ear, you need never wear anything more creative than the basic uniform: people will always remember you.

Multiple piercings make a fashion statement, just what that statement says is yours to decide.

If permanent marks or holes on the body are too much for your idea of fashion, yet you sometimes crave an extreme effect, use your **face** as a canvas. Live out your fantasies with makeup. Develop different families of lip, cheek, and eye colors for different moods—such as mauves, oranges, and reds. Think of your makeup as a painter's palette. You can find inexpensive makeup at chain stores. Woolworth's is rumored to carry a line created by Elizabeth Arden at a fifth of her usual price. If you can find some old magazines, try copying a forties makeup, a fifties makeup, one from the sixties, and the latest face in *Vogue*. Study how they shape, shade, and color the eyes, cheeks, and lips, how they shape the eyebrows; then mix up what looked most striking for your features into your own painted face.

Richard Erker, LaBelle's jewelry designer, has Style.

When you can't afford to play with clothes, you can always have fun dressing up your face.

THE BARGAIN HUNTER

Sophie uses her face as the strongest, most extreme aspect of her appearance. She will never go out in public without having her face done in the palest foundation, her eyes heavily outlined in a smoky gray, and her mouth painted a dark, shiny plum. On other days it will be other colors. Accentuating her strong face will be another strong color, the rich henna shade rinsed into her thick hair. Sophie is known in Paris as one of the most extravagantly dressed women around. Whatever she wears is an original Sophie concoction. She always looks extraordinary on very little money, with a lot of imagination, experimentation, and practice. By trade, she designs textiles and sportswear, and when she's not at the office she's home, compulsively decorating and redecorating her apartment.

Sophie's secret is a willingness to push a look as far as it will go, trusting her eye to find the prize yardage hidden in a stack of mediocre fabrics on sale at the big department stores; trusting her luck to dig up the perfect bits of fur to transform simple cloth into rich exotic gowns, and knit caps into romantic Russian fur clouds floating above her brow.

She always tries to buy everything wholesale, telling manufacturers she's in the trade and hoping they'll sympathize. You can try this in New York or other large garment manufacturing cities on the weekends, or find a friend who has an in with a manufacturer. Clothes are usually half-price, if not less, when bought wholesale.

Sophie makes a masterful use of bits of **fur trim,** adaptable to almost any climate. For instance, in Los Angeles, where it is seldom bone-chillingly cold, a designer cuts striped Mexican serapes into bright, long, conch-belted coats, hangs raccoon tails

The secret shopper: Sofi puts together the most extravagant creations from bits and pieces of sale goods in Paris.

Simple and elegant: plaid on the bias, hanging in large triangles, topped by a babuska and strong makeup.

along the sleeves and the yoked cowboy-style back, then fluffs a fox collar around the neck. There are all sorts of ideas here for transforming a thrift-shop find into a deluxe western look.

The contrast of fur with extreme combinations of fabric and patterns is really arresting, like fur on a soft-flecked wool jersey lined with a check-tablecloth plaid. A seamstress in Paris called Galiana makes odd use of fur by draping the skin of the animal around the front of a coat and down the sleeve, wherever it lands, then stitching it in place. It looks as if some pelt fell out of the sky and just happened to land on the coat. The very primitive treatment of the fur on the tailored wool coat is an odd sight.

One young fashion editor in New York feels you should always take fur to ex-

tremes—use it to further your fantasies rather than just to keep you warm. So she plunked down all her money on a royal blue fox neckpiece on sale at a top furrier instead of opting for a sensible used fur coat from the Ritz Thrift Shop. No one ever forgets those crazy blue foxes nuzzling her neck, and somehow she manages to keep warm. Exaggeration is its own reward.

Larissa Jarzombeck is another New York City fur freak. After coming to New York from Europe, she said, "I had to cope with the overheated apartments and freezing streets. The logical solution was to dress lightly in silk chiffon and wear fur close to

The contrast of fur against day clothes: a bowtie bristles against a warm, puffy old raccoon coat.

the body. Nothing like that was available, so I bought some lamb skins in the fur district and put them together like a jigsaw puzzle. The result was so shocking that for two weeks I dared only to wear it at night!

202 **From feminists to fur freaks, everyone loves Larissa Jarzombeck's jigsaw lambskin coats.**

The first day I ventured into the sunlight, I ran into Miles Davis, who ordered a white one, and later many more. This started a word-of-mouth clientele, mostly musicians and artists." Larissa's coats are sensible, durable, and handsome. Like the royal blue foxes, they are not cheap.

STREETWISE

Marcia approaches a stylized look from the other direction. Instead of furs and luxuries, everything she wears is from a thrift shop, but layered flippantly and combined with ethnic favorites in a really in-

Colette livens up a discreet beige outfit with Indian silk.

Marcia's street chic mixes well-worn thrift shop buys, exotica from abroad, and unexpected layers, then adds a scarf at the neck to tie it all together.

genious way. Everything she wears is tiny, tiny, tiny. She'll wear a miniskirt, for instance, but
• Sling a belted Peruvian bag around the waist, and
• Add silver-trimmed hand-tooled cowboy boots.
To get a couple of lengths going, she'll wear

a mid-calf coat with a tiny waist over the short skirt, and tie a shiny yellow 59¢ Woolworth's scarf in a practiced knot at her neck. Marcia is not trying to tell people she is a lady of luxury; she's telling them she's an independent soul with enough imagination to pull the most disparate bits and pieces into a very personal look. This streetwise look says she's an artist of the first order.

If you study photographs of people who have a finely tuned sense of style, almost invariably you find a **scarf.** Knotted at the neck, draped over a coat, twisted around the head, tied at the waist—scarves show up everywhere. Since fashion magazines often have to show some rather uninspiring dresses manufactured by their major advertisers, they have developed the skill of transforming the ordinary into the exceptional through the use of scarves, belts, and other accessories. Nearly every page of *Vogue* is a lesson in the uses of scarves.

Start up a collection of scarves from thrift shops or Woolworth's and add the cheap cotton squares sold in summer. Try to get different sizes in your favorite colors. Experiment until you feel ready to sink some money into a crepe de Chine square for

203

head wrapping, a silk muffler for the neck, or whatever it is that will give you the most pleasure. The same goes for **belts**—they can change the look of almost any outfit. Try to get as many inexpensive belts as you can find: wide cinch belts in your favorite colors, narrow leather bands that can be worn singly or three at a time, plus an investment belt or two (see Chapter II, Classics).

Perching a **hat** atop your head every morning is a sure way of creating an image. We're not talking about wearing a lot of hats that are in, like a stiff new gaucho hat tied under the chin. We're talking about hats that look better and better as they become more and more you. Some people grow so attached to their hats and their hats to them that they become virtually inseparable;look at Congresswoman Bella Abzug. One of the most original and talented stylists in New York is never seen without his

Make a hat your own by adding a personal touch.

trademark Japanese student cap festooned crown-to-brim with the charms of a decade of friends and travels. He is always dressed in black. All his decorative impulses go into his work and into that extraordinary, glittering, charm-laden cap.

Hats can create and extend an image...in John Wayne's case, it's rough, tough, and very, very tall.

CONSERVATIVE MIX

Andrea Quinn, a fashion editor at *Mademoiselle*, is another person seldom seen without a hat, a man's battered old felt hat with a slouched-down brim. Andrea is as selective and consistent about the clothes she wears as she is about her hat. She wears a very toned down mix of the classics, work clothes, cowboy things, and thrift-shop finds. She prefers old, well-worn clothes to the mania of seasonal fashions she sees covering the market in the showrooms of Seventh Avenue. Her apartment on New York's East Side is a reflection of her understated style: pared down, almost severe, with classic American quilts and bare wooden floors.

Andrea's basic working uniform is jeans and gym T-shirts with two shifts of jewelry, either ethnic things in silver, or gold antiques and family hand-me-downs. "I don't like new clothes very much," she says. "I

used to O. D. on fashion all the time. When I was first a fashion editor, I got a lot of stuff because I could get it half price. But it gets to be too much. Now, if I'm expected to look like a fashion editor then I do, but most of the week I wear very simple things." These are the things that get the most wear in Andrea's closet: Frye boots, St. Laurent boots, cowboy boots, a $6 army-surplus raincoat, an old riding jacket, T-shirts and jeans, a French jeweler's smock, thick sweaters to pile on under the unlined raincoat in the winter, and a collection of old patterned vests she slips on over everything. "It's really weird," says Andrea. "I'm a fashion editor, but I just don't dress myself up much anymore. I've found I like wearing very simple things."

Dalila wears her best fur jacket with second-string classics, gold jewelry, a Cartier watch, and a tight pair of recycled Lee jeans.

Conservative Mix: To one oatmeal linen dress, Andrea adds worn St. Laurent boots, an antique knit vest, beat-up riding jacket and a battered hat from a flea market.

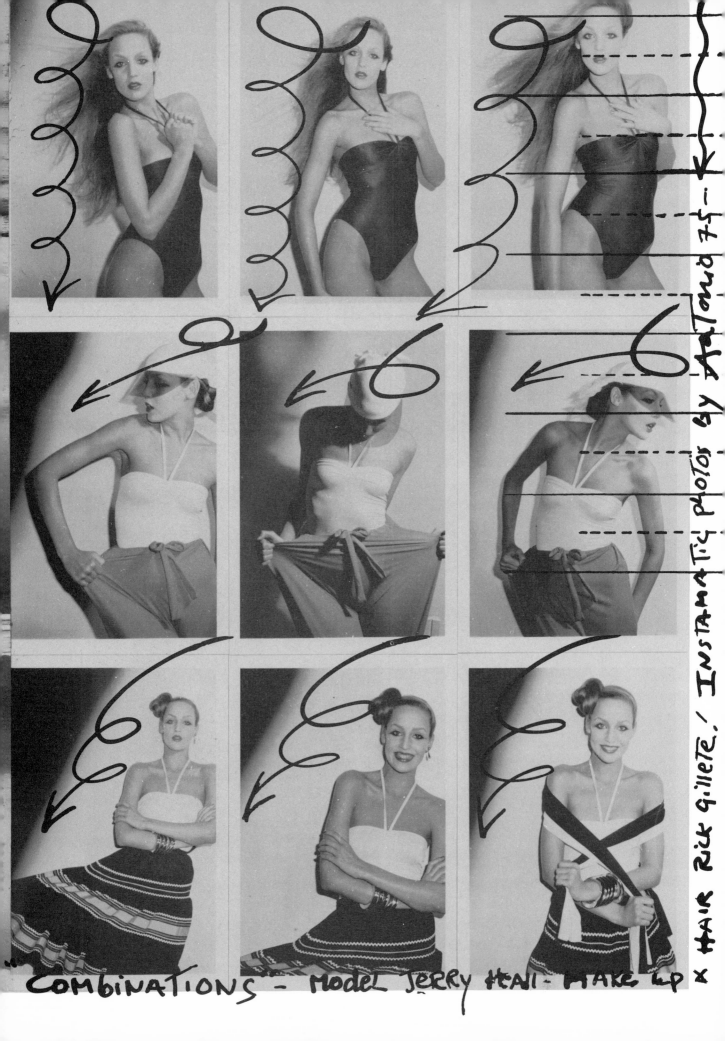

"COMBINATIONS" - MODEL JERRY HALL - MAKE UP & HAIR RICK GILLETE / INSTAMATIC PHOTOS BY JAATORIO 75 - R-

ECLECTIC ELEGANCE

Françoise Kirkland is a lady whose clothes energies go into tops and shoes. Her look is totally eclectic, with an international ring to it. She grew up in Paris and eloped with an American. That was ten years ago, and Françoise still shows that kind of headlong daring in her life and style. Having recently moved from New York to the Hollywood Hills, she is studying journalism at UCLA and developing a new set of thrift-shop contacts.

A typical Eclectic Elegant outfit might combine a bit of everything: wrapping, sports, thrift shops, classics, ethnic, work clothes, basics. Pegged jeans from France with that special tight cut, well-worn suede boots, a $2 Hawaiian print shirt from a rag house bundle, an Isotonic Lycra leotard, and traveler's jewelry: a single earring made from a child's silver bracelet hung with feathers, beads and bits of leather; a silver-studded bracelet from New Delhi; bangles from Morocco; a Cartier tank watch with a

Francoise sports the look of an Angeleno Mixer.

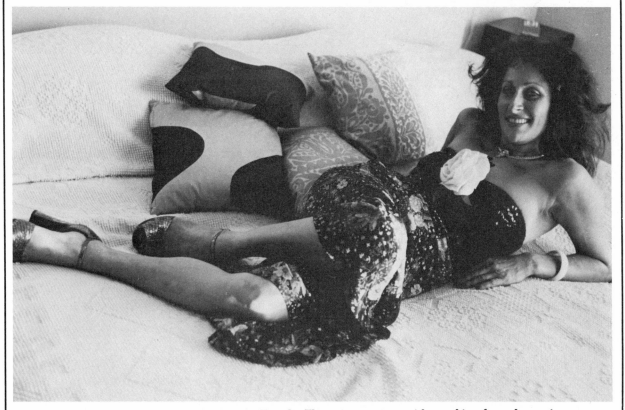

Jazzy day-into-night clothes, left, by Norma Kamali. The suit teams up with anything from drawstring pants to a ruffled evening skirt or all-out Chinese robe glamour. Francoise, above, wears her go-everywhere top.

brown leather band; a bolo tie from Arizona; and a gold chain hung with *figas*, charms from friends, and a childhood St. Christopher's medal.

All this stuff piled up on one person could court disaster, but Françoise puts it together with a practiced eye and a sense of humor:

• The jeans are rolled up over the boots.

• The Hawaiian shirt is knotted in front over the leotard like a calypso dancer's,

• and all the heavy jewelry just seems to fall into place, perhaps because it's all of such quality.

Tune into Soul Train when you're running low on ideas!

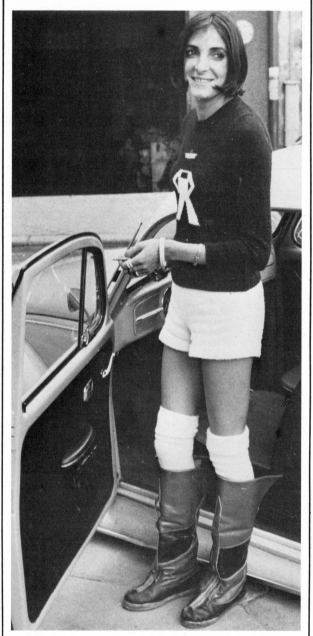

Short, short-shorts, georgeous Tibetan boots (available by mail order), over-the-knee socks: that's imagination.

And Françoise loves wraps. "I make a turban out of this huge piece of tie-dye you just wrap and wrap, whatever way you can manage to keep it on your head! You can also wear it as a sarong skirt. One night I went to Claridge's in London in knickers with the scarf wrapped around my head. The headwaiter said I wasn't allowed in the dining room because I wasn't wearing a skirt. So off I went to the ladies room, took the scarf off my head, and wrapped it into a skirt. They had to let me in!"

Women between eighteen and thirty-five are said to spend over $10 billion on clothes each year. Some of the women in this chapter spend a bit more, and some make a point of spending much less than average. But whichever camp they fall in, they get ten times the mileage and ten times the fun out of their clothes because they've developed their unique talents for making chic from cheap.

Remember: style is about 5% investment and 95% illusion.

THE CHIC SHOPPER'S GUIDE

A directory of stores, flea markets and mail order houses in the U.S., England and France.

Our listings could never be all-inclusive, and regrettably we have missed many excellent stores. Also regrettably some of the stores listed may no longer be in existence as you read this. The purpose of the listings was to give you an idea of what to look for. With this in mind we suggest the following:

Check your local phone book for the address in your town of Goodwill, Salvation Army, Volunteers of America, Catholic Charities, and charitable thrift shops.

Check your newspapers for church, school, and charity rummage sales, flea markets, yard sales, and the like.

Don't overlook the Five and Ten in your town. Woolworth's, McCrory's, and other large chain variety stores offer a wealth of Cheap Chic.

A SMATTERING OF STORES ACROSS THE COUNTRY

BOSTON

Central War Surplus
433-435 Massachusetts Ave.
Boston, Mass.
The place to look for army-navy surplus finds.

CHICAGO

Steve Starr Studios
2654 North Clark St.
Chicago, Ill. 60614
Art Deco, Art Moderne; jewelry, furnishings and accessories.

DALLAS

Beacon Company
4538 McKinney
Dallas, Texas
Check them for utilitarian clothing.

Big Tex Army-Navy Store
215 W. Jefferson
Dallas, Texas
Army-navy surplus items for today's look.

C. R. Adkins Army Store
5800 Maple
Dallas, Texas
And yet another army-navy store to peruse for "finds."

DENVER

Denver Army Store
Denver, Colorado
Here's the place to shop in Denver.

FORT LAUDERDALE

Army-Navy Surplus
700 West Broward Blvd.
Ft. Lauderdale, Fla.
Dash in for a khaki T-shirt to wear as a hot-weather tank top.

HOUSTON

Stelzigs
Houston, Texas
Old, established store carrying Tony Lama boots, Lucchese boots made in San Antonio since 1883 (to order), basic Western clothes and accessories.

Tootsie's
Westheimer Rd. (near the Galleria)
Basic European tops and bottoms; unique accessories.

MILWAUKEE

Goldfish–U.S. Surplus
2103 W. North Ave.
Milwaukee, Wisc.
One of Milwaukee's favorite stores for army-navy surplus.

PEX-U. S. Military Supply
533 West Wisconsin
Milwaukee, Wisc.
Another place to shop in Milwaukee for army-navy needs.

NASHVILLE

Remuda
162 3rd Ave. N.
Nashville, Tenn.
Tops in Western gear, they sell to stores across the country.

PALM BEACH

Palm Beach Thrift Shop
Palm Beach, Florida
Beautiful tailoring, sumptuous beading . . . the impeccable castoffs of the luxury trade.

PHILADELPHIA

Penn Center Army-Navy
20th and Market Sts.
Philadelphia, Pa.
Standard army-navy supples in the heart of Philadelphia.

I. Goldberg's
8th and Chestnut Sts.
Philadelphia, Pa.
Serving University of Pennsylvania students with army-navy surplus for years.

WASHINGTON, D.C.

Sunny's Surplus
3342 M St., N. W.
Georgetown
Washington, D.C.
Georgetown headquarters for
army-navy surplus. Sunny's first
gained fame in Baltimore, Md.,
where they still have a store.

CALIFORNIA

LOS ANGELES AND
SOUTHERN CALIFORNIA

Aardvark's Odd Ark
L. A. (three locations)
Tremendous selection of
used clothes,
generally under $10.

Anne's-tiques
Main Street
Santa Monica
Antiques at excellent prices.

Bun-Ka Do
340 East First St.
L. A.
Amazing selection of
Oriental trinkets.

Crystal Palace
Santa Monica Blvd.
L. A.
Sensational,
expensive costumes.

Ducks Deluxe
Silverlake district
L. A.
Creative jeans,
custom-studded by Bill Shire;
rich assortment of unusual,
special things.

The Flying Emery Board
Beverly Hills
A real investment for
fingernails.

Holly's Harp
Sunset Blvd.
West Hollywood
Sexy, ladylike clothes
in fine silky jersey.

The Hollywood Swap Meet
Santa Monica Blvd. (vacant lot)
West Hollywood
Chic thrift at good prices.

Julian's
3716 Sunset Blvd.
Silverlake, L. A.
Underground ethnic;
gorgeous Chinese jewelry.

Lame Deer Indian Store
8009 Santa Monica Blvd.
L. A.
Western apparel.

Manchee
334 First St.
L. A.
From lovely, tie-dyed
double comforters to *geta*
sandals on stilts.

Mehitabel
3716 Sunset Blvd.
Silverlake, L. A.
Scarves and cottons from India;
exotic beads and amulets—
all at reasonable prices.

Miss Amber
426 W. 7th St.
L. A.
6640 Hollywood Blvd.
Hollywood
Flash and dazzle;
first with English scarf dresses.

Ola Hudson
Melrose
West Hollywood
The funky forties
feel, custom designed.

The Orient
6626 Hollywood Blvd.
Hollywood
Real finds; cotton and silk
kimonos hidden among
the standard tourist items.

Oriental Arts
325 First St.
L. A.
Antique Orientalia in brass,
bronze, and cloisonnés.

Oriental Silk Company
8365 Beverly Blvd.
L. A.
Beautiful silk fabrics,
robes, scarves, crocheted tops.
Send for catalog.

Pillars of Eagle Rock
Eagle Rock (near East L. A.)
The Loehman's of the West—
designer clothes at
less than half price.

Surplus Marts
6263 Santa Monica Blvd.
(corner Vine)
L. A.
Army-navy surplus.

SAN FRANCISCO
AND THE BAY AREA

Abbe's
1420 Clement St.
S. F.
Antique and secondhand clothes.
Most look new and barely worn.

Carousel Resale Shop
1642A Irving St.
S. F.
Used clothing with sensational
buys from the thirties.

Casey's Faded World
2265 Upper Market
S. F.
Embroidered kimonos and
satin acetate lingerie.

Coastside Corral
Oddstad Blvd.
Pacifica
Full line of Western gear.

French's Hitching Post
1205 Third St.
San Rafael
Shop for Western wear.

Green's Boot & Saddle Shop
12153 San Pablo Ave.
Richmond
Another "don't miss" for Western.

Janan Resale Fashions
1432 California
S. F.
Buys on secondhand
designer clothes and shoes.

Kaplan's Surplus & Sporting Goods
1055 Market nr. 7th
S. F.
Check for army-navy surplus
and utilitarian looks.

New Ideal
1336 Grand
S. F.
Clothing for men and women,
all organized by racks.
No fitting rooms, good buys.

Next-to-New Shop
2226 Fillmore St.
S. F.
Operated by the Junior League—
terrific for classics.

Obiko
3924 Sacramento
S. F.
Expensive, unusual jewelry;
unique designer clothes;
satin shoes from Hong Kong.

The Palace Museum
1546 Polk St.
S. F.
Elegant funk, specializing in
recycled clothing made from
old jeans.

Robert Kirk Ltd.
150 Post St.
S. F.
Tops in men's classics.
Send for catalog.

Ron Richards Saddlery
2510 Telegraph Ave.
Oakland
Wide selection of Western wear.

Second Hand Rose
3326 23rd St.
S. F.
Fantastic emporium
where you can find racks of
antique and period clothes.

The Street Shop
4100 19th St.
S. F.
Best for used men's wear—
lots of quality at bargain prices.

NEW YORK

Abercrombie & Fitch
Madison Ave. & 45th St.
Also branches; for catalog and
address of the Abercrombie's
near you write:
    Abercrombie & Fitch
    P. O. Box 4266
    Grand Central Station
    N.Y.C. 10017
A sportsman's Brooks Brothers:
similar Ivy League style.
Shell bags, game bags, leather
suitcases, and classics for
both men and women.

Albert Hosiery Stores
Eight branches in Manhattan
Full line of Danskin leotards
and tights.

Alexander's
731 Lexington Ave. (at 58th St.)
Department store known for
designer copies and inexpensive
European imports.

American Indian Arts Center
1042 Madison Ave. (at 79th St.)
Contemporay conch silver belts
and handcrafted jewelry of
collector's quality.

Anne's Dressmaking & Alterations
1020 Lexington Ave. (at 73rd St.)
249-1372
A name and number to have
for custom dressmaking,
alterations, etc.

Appleby's
146 West 4th St.
They feature factory seconds on
jeans: new $3.99; washed $2.99.

Arden's
1014 Sixth Ave. (near 38th St.)
Knit cloches, broad-brimmed
velours in many colors and
broad-brimmed straw hats,
all at low prices.

Army & Navy Supply Store
Third Ave. at 107th St.
Army surplus and lots of
good work clothes.

Artbag
735 Madison Ave.
Mail in your worn but classic bag
for an estimate for repairs.
They give a one-year guarantee
on all work.

Azuma
415 Fifth Ave., and branches
Cotton scarves, straw hats,
cotton skirts, blouses, dresses.
Straw slippers: 39¢.

Beckenstein Woolens
125 Orchard St.
Fine woolens, men's suiting.

Bogie's Antique Furs
201 East 10th St.
Antique furs and clothes, with
new bundles arriving twice weekly.

Bottega Veneta
Madison Ave.
Silk squares of crepe de Chine
from Milan; beautiful leather goods
and bags for people who don't
need designer's initials.

Brooks Brothers
346 Madison Ave. (at 44th St.)
and branches
The store for American classics.
Send for catalog and for the
location of store near you.

Budget Uniform Center
110 East 59th St.
Lab coats, nursing and waitress
uniforms. Large selection of
hospital "scrub" clothes for dyeing
which can only be purchased
by the dozen.

Camp & Trail
Park Place (near City Hall)
Clothes for the
Field and Stream effect.

Center Thrift Shop
120 East 28th St.
Some things priced, some not.
If you're in the neighborhood
it's worth a stop.

Charleston Market
21 Second Ave.
A huge selection of thirties clothes.

Cherchez
141 East 76th St. (upstairs)
Beautiful Victorian camisoles,
slips, dresses for summer;
in perfect condition.

Chinese Emporium
154 West 57th St.
Utilitarian Chinese workers'
jackets, other items from China.

Chipp
14 East 44th St.
Full line of traditional,
English-oriented men's clothes.

Chocolate Soup
249 East 77th St.
Darling children's clothes;
also the mail order Danish
schoolbag that's a great carryall.

Chor Bazaar
801 Lexington Ave.
A wide selection of
cotton muslin scarves, dresses.

Conscious Decision
4th St. off the Bowery
Thermal underwear with silkscreen
designs, assorted sweatshirts in
various colors, and sportswear.

Dan's Trading Post
302 West 49th St.
A fine Western shop.

Delores Harrison
825 Columbus Ave. (near 100th St.)
(663-0389)
Did alterations at St. Laurent's
Rive Gauche. Dresses begin at $25
(with you providing the material),
slacks for $10.

Diamond's Secondhand
Clothes, Inc.
42 Hester St.
Every day but Saturday. Caters to
men only. All suits are marked
"fair," "good," or "excellent," and
range from $1 to $30.

Double Dealers Ltd.
1364 Lexington Ave.
Children's resale store. They
will take your children's
outgrown clothes and sell them
on consignment. Clothing is
in excellent condition.

Dudley Eldridge
39 West 32nd St.
Custom-made shirts.

Early Halloween
180 Ninth Ave.
They carry a wide selection
of old clothes, old shoes, and
wonderful suspenders.

Echo Scarf Co.
485 Fifth Ave.
(682-5430)
Write or phone for store near you
that carries their 27-in. square,
white, thin handkerchief
cotton scarf, $5.

El Mercado
510 Broome St. (in Soho)
Mexican sweaters and blankets—
very warm, a little scratchy.
Reasonable prices.

Encore Resale Dress Shop
1132 Madison Ave. (at 84th St.)
Where the local upper-East-Siders
take their year-old designer
clothes. Reasonable prices
considering what you're buying.
All clothes like new.

Everybody's Thrift Shop
9th Ave. and 56th St.
Some of the most well-heeled
New Yorkers donate their clothes
to the ten charities represented
at this shop.

Farkas and Kovacs, Inc.
1187 Lexington Ave.
The most exquisite custom-made
shoes for men and women at
prices to match.

Folio
888 Madison Ave.
Carries all sorts of little books
and notepapers. Makes up
beautiful calling cards with your
choice of fifty designs.

Forty's Wink Antique
Fashion Boutique
1331A Third Ave.
Good assortment of antiques
and children's clothes.

Freshwater Mfg. Inc.
716 Broadway (at 4th St.)
Used blue jeans, fatigues, sailor
pants, army-navy overcoats.
Old dresses, coats, scarves, and
new T-shirts in a rainbow
of colors.

The Frugal Frog
1707 Second Ave. (near 88th St.)
Thrift shop for children with
amusements for the children while
the mothers shop.

Gladstone Fabrics
56th St.
Carries many fabrics from the
forties and fifties. They will match
a color swatch for $7, no matter
how much fabric you need.

Gyro Surplus Corp.
Broadway & Bleeker St.
Large supply of work clothes.

Happiness Thrift Shop
1444 Third Ave.
Run for the benefit of the United
Cerebral Palsy of New York.

Harriet Love
128 West 13th St.
Harriet has an elegant selection
of Victorian capes, shawls, dresses,
lace blouses, and nightgowns with
tiny tucks, lace edging. She also
carries antique jewelry.

Henri Bendel
10 West 57th St.
Take in Zandra Rhodes's dresses,
and train your eye with the best of
European ready-to-wear. Shoe Biz
has the best, most stylish, shoes
in New York.

Herbert Dancewear
1657 Broadway
Full line of Danskin dance supplies
and also Herbert Economy
leotards, tights, and skirts.
Send for catalog.

Herman's
15 West 38th St.
Well-made hats at reasonable
prices: velour, beaver, straw, or
fabric from about $10 to $15.
Ribbons, flowers, and feathers
to choose for a personal touch.

Hornblower Antiques
Canal St. and West Broadway
A good place for used clothing.

Hudson's
Third Ave at 13th St.
Army surplus but often jammed
and ill-mannered help. Brown
leather motorcycle jackets and a
large stock of jeans and
work clothes.

Jackie Rogers for Men
27 East 67th St.
Men's clothing, many imports,
excellent taste at inflated prices.

Jean Warehouse
Branches throughout Manhattan
Jeans, skirts and T-shirts.
Inexpensive with a contemporary,
fashion-conscious look.

Jenny Waterbags
150 East 19th St.
Women's and men's pants
made to order plus ready-made,
one-of-a-kind clothes.

Jerri's Shoe Outlet
2611 Broadway (near 98th St.)
Very good Greek boots, and shoes
carried by Bendel's, but much
cheaper here.

Jezebel
265 Columbus Ave.
Antique clothes in good condition.
It would be much cheaper
out of New York, but . . .

Joe's Army-Navy
163 Orchard St.
Army-navy surplus downtown.

Kasoundra Kasoundra
(777-9851, by appointment)
One-of-a-kind, handmade,
patchwork clothes of unusual
fabrics. Crocheted Art Nouveau-ish
handbags in antique frames
touched here and there with
butterflies, birds, beads, and
lined in velvet.

Kaufman's
139 East 24th St.
They carry everything for the
rider and Midnight Cowboy.

Kaufman Surplus & Arms
Broadway & Houston St.
Jeans, army surplus, and
work clothes.

Kaufman—The Gun Room
319 West 42nd St.
Lee jeans, army surplus, and
work clothes.

Kavala Imports, Inc.
45 Christopher St.
(near Sheridan Square)
Greek cotton skirts, tops, and
caftans; crocheted cotton tops
and skirts.

Kip's Bay Boys Club Thrift Shop
1577 Third Ave.
Worth a stop as you tour
the Third Ave. thrift shops.

Larrissa
484 Broome St. (second floor)
Fur coats, worn inside-out so the
fur is next to your body.

The Leader
305 West 125th St.
Army surplus and
work clothes uptown.

Mexican Art Annex
23 West 56th St.
Cotton tunic shirts, skirts,
and scarves.

Michael's Resale
1041 Madison Ave. (at 79th St.)
Great buys on designer clothes;
all in excellent condition.

Miller's
123 East 24th St.
Horsy-set central. Jeans, jodhpurs,
riding boots, everything.

Moonstone Gallery
498 Hudson St.
255-8714 (phone for hours)
Clothing, jewelry. Expensive.

Moroccan Fashion & Art, Ltd.
818 Third Ave.
Importers of Moroccan and
Tunisian classics such as solid
black capes, cotton hooded jackets,
leather gold-embossed slippers.

The Nearly New Thrift Shop
54th St. at Ninth Ave.
A well-heeled group gives
donations here, so keep trying.

Neighborhood Thrift Shop
449 Second Ave. (near 25th St.)
The last Monday of each month
is sale day—half price for
everything on the racks.

The New World Gift Shoppe
906 Madison Ave. (near 73rd St.)
    and
1131 Amsterdam Ave.
near (116th St.)
Oriental garments, jewelry, and gifts

Odyssey House Thrift Boutique
861 Third Ave. (near 52nd St.)
Shoes are the hottest item right
now, both used and new. There are
also a number of new clothes
that sell for about 40 percent less
than they would in typical boutiques.

Ohrbach's
5 West 34th St.
Department store with designer
copies and inexpensive European
imports, as well as masses of
inexpensive merchandise.

O Mistress Mine
143 Seventh Ave. South
New and old dresses, long or short
jean skirts, overall skirts, jackets
from old quilts, old furs, much,
much more and always changing.
It's their policy to underprice.

Opportunity Shop
46 West 47th St.
Perhaps the largest thrift shop
of all, with two selling floors and
four additional storage floors
feeding in every day.

O'Susanna
134 East 17th St.
All sorts of old, real Japanese
kimonos; exotic Japanese makeup
and a knowledgeable makeup
artist, Susanna.

Planned Parenthood Thrift Shop
324 East 59th St.
Good variety of children's clothes.
Theatrical and antique clothes
are another feature.

Propinquity
243 Third Ave. (near 20th St.)
Pretty antique costumes as well
as Bette Wanderman's own designs
using antique fabrics. Some unique
items like an elaborate wedding
dress are rentable.

Resale Shop
802 Lexington Ave. (62nd St.)
High quality, low quantity,
pleasant help.

Richards Army-Navy Authentics
233 West 42nd St.
Army-surplus classics in an
exciting area.

Ridge Antique Furs
33 West 8th St.
    and
Warehouse at 55 Great Jones St.
For years a favorite of chic
New Yorkers with little money.
Their fur coats range in quality
from tattered to perfection. Also
fur pillows, rugs, muffs, etc.

Ritz Thrift Shop
107 West 57th St.
Use your old fur as a trade-in if it's
in good condition. Ritz will fit,
process, clean, and glaze your
purchase free, with unlimited free
storage and minor repairs.

Rive Gauche
855 Madison Ave.
St. Laurent's ready-to-wear line
carried here and at
Bloomingdale's.

Rosza Glenn
1546 Second Ave. (near 80th St.)
(535-9615)
Dressmaker, starts at $10 for
minor remodeling.

Salvation Army (main branch)
536 West 46th St.
This is thrift-shop central.

Search 'n Save Thrift Shop
1465 Third Ave. (near 83rd St.)
Boxes of new children's and adults'
clothing at ridiculously low prices.
Ask to see the more expensive
clothing and furs.

Second Act
1046 Madison Ave. (near 80th St.)
Children's resale shop with a
good selection, more for girls than
boys. Shoes, boots, records, and
books on sale too.

Sermoneta
740 Madison Ave.
South American market goods at
low prices. Wicker and clothes.

Simons
67 Third Ave. at 4th St.
Work clothes of all manufacturers.

SoHo Canal Flea Market
369 Canal St. (near West Broadway)
An indoor and outdoor market,
open year round, seven days from
11 A.M. to 6 P.M., for antiques,
clothes, and collectibles.

Sona
55th St. (between Fifth &
Madison Aves.)
Indian clothing.
See Paris.

South Asia Gift
848 Broadway (near 14th St.)
Martial arts supplies, Kung Fu
shoes and uniforms, karate ghis.

Spectrum Imports, Inc.
2121 Broadway (near 75th St.)
Third floor
Mexican sweaters in natural and
colors for $30; children's, $17.

Stitching Horse, Inc.
156 East 64th St. (Lexington Ave.)
Frye boots and handmade Stewart
cowboy boots from Arizona.
Send for free catalog.

St. Marks Leather Co.
37 St. Marks Place
Frye and Durango boots.

Stuyvesant Square Thrift Shop
1430 Third Ave. (at 81st St.)
Big, airy sales floor, good supply of
furs and better women's clothes.

Sun Hi's Gift Co.
126 7th Ave. (between 17th
and 18th Sts.)
Oriental gowns, lounge robes,
Hoppi coats and beautiful padded
bright cotton jackets from China.

Sweet-Orr & Co., Inc.
1290 Ave. of the Americas
Overalls, work clothes, outerwear.
Write to them for the stores nearest
you.

Tepee Town
Port Authority Building
8th Ave. and 40th St.
        also
42nd St. near Fifth Ave.
Indian jewelry and embossed
leather bags, wallets, and belts.

Thrift House
39 West 57th St.
Offers delicious outfits at prices
well below many of the other
thrift shops.

T. O. Day
509 Fifth Avenue (near 42nd St.)
8th Floor
Shoe and boot remodeling. Will
blunt or round off pointed toes,
change closed shoes to sandals,
change heel height and width.

Union Shirt Company, Inc.
915 Broadway
Makers of the West Point shirt.

Weiss & Mahoney
142 Fifth Avenue
Send for mail-order catalog which
lists almost every imaginable army-
surplus item down to women's
dress uniforms. The best all-around
assortment at the lowest prices.

West Side Warehouse
2248 Broadway (at 81st St.)
They deal in recycled patches of
jeans reshaped to your
measurements as a skirt or as
patched denim pants.

EUROPE AND MEXICO

ENGLAND

Badges & Equipment
London
Real English army/navy/RAF
surplus including flying suits,
paratrooper trousers,
jungle hats, and more.

Biba
Kensington High St.
London
London's most style-conscious
department store.

Brixton Market
(The Electric Mile)
London
Every day except Wednesday.
West Indian goods, used clothing.

Bus Stop
(near Biba)
London
Up-to-the-minute designs
by Lee Bender.

Chelsea Cobbler
London
Custom or ready-made boots—
long lasting, expensive classics.
Similar shop in New York.

The Frock Exchange
450 Fulham Road
London
Sells secondhand quality clothes
including Ossie Clark, more.

Jean Machine
London
Jeans, baseball T-shirts,
sweatshirts.

Laurence Corner
62 Hampstead Rd.
London
Genuine army/navy surplus.

Lobb
London
Tops for men's shoes.
See also Paris.

Lonsdale Sports
London
For sport uniforms—
striped jerseys, rugby shorts,
football socks.

Marks & Spencer
London
Large department store, great for
sweaters and children's clothes.

Oxfam
War on Want
Red Cross
London
Especially good thrift shop
for old dresses.

Portobello Road Market
London
Street market open Friday and
Saturday; Saturday is the best.
Antiques, clothing, and
lots more to see.

Turnbull & Asser
London
Men's shirts custom and ready
made. Striped silks, soft cottons.
These shirts carried by
Bonwit Teller in the U.S.A.

Westaway & Westaway
London
Across from the British Museum.
Cashmere sweaters at a low price
in all styles and colors.

Zapata
London
Elegantly designed, expensive
shoes by Manolo Blahnik.

FRANCE

A la Blouse des Halles
140, rue de Faubourg St. Martin
Paris 75010
Coveralls, jewelers' smocks,
and butchers' jackets—plus more.

Au Bon Marche
20–38, rue de Sevres
Paris 75006
A department store
worth looking into.

B. H. V. (Bazaar de l'Hotel de Ville)
rue de Rivoli, Paris 75001
rue de Flandres, Paris 75019
Department store with a large
selection of utilitarian clothes.

C et A
124, rue de Rivoli and
Centre Commercial Tour
Montparnasse
Raincoats, parkas, and rain suits.

Candide
4, rue de Miromesnil
Paris
Very elegant, creamy lingerie.

Compagnie Francaise
de l'Orient et de la Chine
Faubourg St. Honoré &
Blvd. St. Germaine
Paris
Crisscross, antislip gloves,
all sorts of oriental delights.

Dilidam
127, rue St. Denis
Paris
Good supply of
fifties raincoats, sweaters.

Eres
2, rue Tronchet
Paris
Warm-up suits in
five different colors.

Estelle
115, rue St. Denis
Paris
The specialty is jewelry.

Fernand Gontarski
3, rue Gaston-Oarboyx
Paris
For cowboy boots in Paris.

Galeries Lafayette
Bd. Hausmann
Paris 75009 and
Centre Maine-Montparnasse
Paris 75015
Well-known department store
for just about everything.

Globe (The Khaki Rush)
12, rue Pierre Lescot
Paris
Army clothes, Chinese and
Japanese workers' pants and
kimonos, newest looks from
old favorites.

La Grande Truanderie
111, rue St. Denis
Paris
Assortment of romantic dresses.

Indian Trading Post
Passage Choiseul
Paris
For American Indian/Western
gear in Paris.

INNO (4 locations)
Inno Passy; 53, rue de Passy;
Inno Montparnasse;
31, rue du Depart;
Inno Nation; 4-5, rue de la Plaine;
Hyper-Inno; Viry-Chatillon (93)
One of France's many good
variety/chain stores.

Jean Bazaar
Paris
All the American workclothes
cut to fit French hips.

Lobb
Paris (also London)
Best custom shoes in the Western
world, according to all reports.

Madame Cadolle
14, rue Cambon
Paris
Fine example of French lingerie.

La Maison Bleue
rue Pierre-Lescot
Paris
Brushed cotton flannelette dresses,
skirts, trousers, hats, etc.

Marche Aux Puces
(street markets in Paris)
Marche St. Pierre—good selection
of fabrics, old and new
Montmartre
Porte St. Ouen
Mairie de Montreuil—
good bargains; arrive by 7 A.M.

Messageries
6, rue St. Denis
Paris
Best of all the new shops in the
former Les Halles market area.

Mode Frisson
Paris
Best shoes in Paris, next to Tilbury,
in the classic mode.

Monoprix
Bd. Hausmann
Paris
and other locations
throughout France.
Similar to American Woolworth's,
but with more selection in clothing,
plus better style and quality.

Passe Simple
25, rue St. Denis
Paris
Thirties through fifties
clothes and jeans.

Printemps
Bd. Hausmann
Paris 75009
Another great French
department store.

Prisunic
Paris, several locations; and
throughout France.
Variety/chain store that's
especially good for baby and
children's basic wardrobes.

La Redoute
Roubaix
Paris
Great French catalog, similar to
American Sears Roebuck.

Repetto
Place de L'Opera
Paris
French equivalent of Capezio.
Ballet supplies, leotards, etc.
Excellent "off-color" selection.

La Samaritaine
Pont Neuf et Bd. des Capucines
Paris
Sensational selection of overalls,
painters' and jewelers' smocks,
electricians' jackets, nurses'
uniforms.

Soldes magazine
3, Place Malesherbes
Paris 75017
Send for this—every month it lists
the best bargains in each of
Paris's twenty districts, with
emphasis on unique, quality items.

Sona
400, rue St. Honore
Paris (also New York)
Special is saris in cotton or
hand-painted silk.

Sotovol
125, rue du Faubourg St. Martin
Paris
Ideal for jumpsuits. They cater to
racing car drivers, aviators, etc.

Thiery
45, rue Caumartin
Paris
Men's pants in polyester/wool
in all colors from $13 up.

Tilbury
St. Germain
Paris
The best women's shoes in Paris.

Les Trois Quartiers
Bd. de la Madeleine
Paris 75001
Old style quality at popular prices.

Yankee (3 locations)
24, rue de la Boetie, Paris 8
39, rue de Jussieu
(opposite the university) Paris 5
56, Bd. de Rochechouart, Paris 18
American surplus in Paris with
a French touch; khaki boots made
to order. American jeans, all makes.

L'Echoppe
4, rue de l'Observance
84 Carpentras
Vaucluse
Antique clothing from the
Provençal region of France.

ITALY

Basile
Milan
Some of the best men's tailoring
in Italy; also beautiful women's
clothing. Expensive but lasting.

Carano
Milan
A selection of the best shoes in
Italy; also Yves St. Laurent boots.

Fendi
Milan
Beautiful, luxurious unlined
fur coats.

MEXICO

Casa Canal
        and
Casa Maxwell
San Miguel de Allende
Both carry traditional Mexican
clothes of the first quality, and
will also do custom dresses
for a moderate price.

SPAIN

Loewe's
35 Paseo de Gracia
Barcelona
Best shop for leather goods—
top quality but top prices.

MAIL ORDER AND CATALOG

Acadian Crafts Association
P. O. 29
St. Caterine Street
Madawaski, Maine 04756
Hand crocheted French-Acadian
crafts—ladies' wear and infant's
clothing. Well priced.

Action and Leisure
45 East 30th St.
N. Y. C. 10016
Patrick shoes from France in bright
colors. Soccer, tennis, training,
track, cycling, ski, and rugby shoes.

A. S. Cooper & Sons, Ltd.
No. 37 Front St.
Hamilton, Bermuda
Classic shetland crew-neck sweaters
in fifteen colors. Other classics.

Bates Industries, Inc.
700 West 16th St.
Long Beach
California 90801
Leather motorcycle garments
including custom leather
motocross pants.

Budget Uniform Center, Inc.
1613 Chestnut St.
Philadelphia, Pa. 19103
Sixty-page color catalog mailed
three times a year. Uniforms in
white and colors; jackets, lab coats,
etc.

Capezio Dance Catalog
1841 Broadway
N. Y. C.
Full line of dance clothes and
accessories. Ask also for the store
nearest you.

Casler
Box 1070
Ontario, Canada 91762
Heavy-duty padded denim
motocross pants, other riding gear.

Castello
836 Broadway
N. Y. C. 10003
Send for fencing equipment catalog
or combative sports catalog . . .
judo coats, Kung Fu suits, etc.

Danskin, Inc.
1114 Avenue of the Americas
New York City 10036
Tops, bodysuits, hosiery, and
dancewear for men, women, and
children. Also ask for the store
in your area.

Empire
443 Broadway
N. Y. C. 10013
Fifties leather jackets, chenille
emblems, all sorts of uniforms.

Everlast Sport
750 East 132nd St.
Bronx, N.Y. 10454
Boxing equipment, including shorts
and robes.

Frederick's of Hollywood
6608 Hollywood Blvd.
Hollywood, Calif.
Longtime mail-order leader in "sexy
chic" . . . worth reading, even if you
don't order. Had perhaps the first
"string" bathing suits; lots more.

Greek Island Ltd.
215 East 49th St.
N. Y. C.
Cotton voile or gauze scarves;
cotton tops, skirts, and caftans.

GSC Athletic Equipment
600 North Pacific Ave.
San Pedro
Calif. 90733
Gymnastics clothes and equipment
of all sorts. A school supplier.

Healthways
P. O. Box 45055
Los Angeles
Calif. 90045
Scuba and diving gear including
knives that strap on your ankle or
upper arm. Ask also for store in
your area.

Holubar
Dept. 4-119H Box 7
Boulder, Colorado 80302
Down jackets and parkas, also
duffel bags.

House of Morgan
Box 789
Big Spring, Texas
Western suits for men and women.
Also Rio of Mercedes custom boots.

The Irish-Thai Company
P. O. Box 2
Arlington, Massachusetts
They import Umbro Sportswear,
real soccer uniforms made in
England.

J. Capps & Sons, Ltd.
11800 Sunrise Valley Drive
Reston, Virginia 22091
Body-armor disguised as vests,
sport coats, T-shirts, etc. Just the
thing for revolutions.

J. C. Penney Co., Inc.
1301 Avenue of the Americas
N. Y. C. 10019
Big fall and spring catalogs. Best in men's and boys' denim jeans, work clothes, and women's blouses.

Joe Hall Boots
P. O. Box 17971
El Paso, Texas
Fine Western boots made to order with custom details.

Johnson North Star Hockey Equipment
1900 North Springfield Avenue
Chicago, Ill. 60647
Everything you would ever want to know about suiting up for hockey.

Kawasaki Accessories
1062 McGaw
Santa Ana, Calif. 92705
Motorcycling clothes of great style, some made by Hang-Ten.

L. L. Bean, Inc.
Freeport, Maine 04032
100 percent wool plaid shirts, wool jackets, everything you'll ever need for the outdoor, sportive life. Over one hundred pages of heaven!

Miller's
Mail Order Division
P. O. Box 720
Canal Street Station
N.Y.C. 10013
Western and English riding clothes and equipment; beautiful riding jackets, classic boots. Cost of catalog, $1.

Miller Stockman
Box 5407
Denver, Colorado 80217
Comprehensive shop-at-home catalog of men's and women's Western wear.

Montgomery Ward
Chicago, Ill. 60607
You must place an order first to get the catalog. Good buys in sports and work clothes.

Neiman-Marcus Co.
Dallas, Texas 75201
Christmas catalog is the big one . . . a rich man's "wish book." Small charge for Christmas catalog, but worth it for the reading.

Nudie's Rodeo Tailors
5015 Lankershim Blvd.
North Hollywood, Calif.
Ultimate in flashy Western wear. Custom tailor to the stars of the Grand Ole Opry as well as rock 'n roll. Extraordinary boots, too.

Nocona Boot Company
P. O. Box 599
Nocona, Texas 76255
Brochure of cowboy boots and the name of your local dealer.

Norman Kung-Fu Karate
6362 Stanton
Philadelphia, Pa. 19138
Inexpensive martial arts uniforms.

Norm Thompson
1805 N. W. Thurman
Portland, Oregon 97209
First quality, outdoorsy classics for men and women.

Robert Kirk, Ltd.
150 Post St.
San Francisco, Calif. 94108
Catalog of men's classics.

Sears-Roebuck, Inc.
Chicago, Ill.
Comprehensive shop-at-home catalogs; big fall and spring books.

Sebago, Inc.
Westbrook, Maine 04092
Sebago's "Dockside" is a handsewn, elk-tanned cowhide moccasin with a nonslip sole. Write for the store nearest you.

The Slipper House
1450 Ala Moana Blvd.
Honolulu, Hawaii 96814
Over one hundred slippers, thongs, gaza straw thongs, Lauhala slippers, and more. Most under $10.

Sperry Top-Sider
18 Rubber Avenue
Naugatuck, Conn. 06770
Topsider moccasins for boating, etc. Elk-tanned, dry to original softness.

Sportote
P. O. Box 160
Mukwonago, Wisconsin 53149
Light, bright, canvas handled team bags in nylon or canvas.

Stall & Dean Uniforms
99 Church Street
Brockton, Massachusetts 02403
Baseball uniforms from socks to caps.

Tex Tan Western Leather Co.
Box 711
Yoakum, Texas 77995
Western accessories and gifts including belts, hand-tooled wallets, bags, silver-and-gold rodeo trophy buckles.

Tibetan Arts & Crafts Ltd.
693 Madison Ave.
N. Y. C.
Tibetan shoes and wonderful pointed toe boots; fur and wool hats with earflaps, fabrics, sweaters, coats, and more.

Tony Lama
P. O. Drawer 9518
El Paso, Texas 79985
Write for the name of a store in your area that carries his extraordinary line of cowboy boots in all leathers and styles.

Treasures of Asia
13 East 30th St.
N. Y. C.
Cotton cowboy shirts and safari jackets for men and women.

U. S. Sports
82525 South Monroe
Houston, Texas 77017
Norstar motocross boots; manufactured in Italy by Munari.

Webco
Box 429
Venice, Calif. 90291
116 page catalog for $1.50. Padded denim motocross jeans, full range of motorcycle gear.

Western Brands
P. O. Box 1880
Estes Park, Colorado 80517
Mail-order Levi's, moccasins, scout boots, buckskin trousers and shirts, leather shoulder bags, and all sorts of unique leather items.

Wrangler
c/o Blue Bell
1411 Broadway
N. Y. C.
Write to them for the store in your area that carries Wranglers.

Yankee Motor Company
Box 36
Schenectady, N.Y. 12301
Full-bore black motorcycle street boots made in Italy, motocross boots with folding cam-type buckles; Agostini touring boots.

THE CARE AND FEEDING OF FABRICS

	COTTON	WOOL	SILK	SYNTHETICS
DESCRIPTION:	Natural fiber that's versatile, durable—launders well.	Natural fiber with insulating capacity—can be warm or cool.	Natural fiber that is expensive but dyes well, has natural luster and strength.	Many varieties that duplicate natural fibers, some are unique.
VARIETIES: (Types listed are but a few, those most mentioned in this book.)	Batiste, Calico, Cheesecloth, Corduroy, Denim, Gauze, Flannelette, Lawn, Madras, Muslin, Oxford, Velour, Velveteen.	Camel hair, Cashmere, Cavalry twill, Challis, Flannel, Gabardine, Herringbone, Melton, Mohair Tweed.	Chiffon, China silk, crepe de Chine, Georgette, Satin, Mousseline de Soie, Shantung, Velvet.	Acetate, Acrylic, Nylon, Polyester, Rayon and Spandex. Generally known under brand names as Orlon, Dacron, Fortrell, Kodell, etc.
CARE:	Hand-launders well. If pre-shrunk may be machine washed (depending on type). Iron with hot iron or not at all, i.e., terrycloth, seersucker.	Dry clean most items but may be washed in cold water with special detergent such as Woolite. Protect against moths.	Dry cleaning is recommended for most items but some can be carefully hand laundered in cool water. Protect from long exposure to light.	Care requirements vary, so for best results follow manufacturer's instructions carefully.

STAINS:	MACHINE- AND HAND-WASHABLES	OTHER FABRICS
BLOOD	Soak in lukewarm water and enzyme-containing pre-soak or detergent. Launder.	Treat with cold water plus 2 tablespoons per quart table salt solution. Rinse and blot with towel.
CHEWING GUM	Remove gum from surface with a dull knife. Soak affected area in cleaning fluid. Launder.	Same as for washable fabrics, but do not launder.
CHOCOLATE OR COFFEE	Soak in warm water with enzyme-containing product. Launder.	If fabric is colorfast, sponge with lukewarm water.
GREASE AND TAR	Place towel under stain. Pour cleaning fluid through stained area. Launder in hot water.	Take to dry cleaner. Identify stain for dry cleaner's information.
MAKEUP	Soak overnight in warm detergent solution containing 4 tablespoons household ammonia to each quart of water. Rinse. Launder. Bleach if necessary.	Take to dry cleaner. Identify stain for dry cleaner's information.
MILDEW	Launder with detergent and chlorine bleach if color and fabric permit.	Take to dry cleaner. Identify stain for dry cleaner's information.
PERSPIRATION	Launder with detergent in hot water. Bleach if necessary.	Sponge with water if fabric is colorfast.

Note on Linen: Once widely used for summer apparel because of its high moisture absorption, linen is fast being replaced by synthetics. A garment of real linen would classify as an investment today. To its advantage, linen is smooth and therefore does not lint and can be washed or dry cleaned, depending on dye, finish, design application, and garment construction. To its disadvantage, linen wrinkles very easily. For best results, it is wise to iron with a very hot iron and avoid pressing into sharp creases.

INDEX

Page references in italics indicate captions or illustrations.

PHOTOGRAPHIC AND ILLUSTRATIVE CREDITS